THE BEGINNER'S GUIDE TO RAISING CHICKENS

FEED AND WATER, HEALTH CARE, BACKYARD ACTIVITIES, AND SO MUCH MORE FOR MEAT & LAYING CHICKENS, CHICKS, AND ROOSTERS. BUILDING A BACKYARD HOMESTEAD AND RAISING CHICKENS IS MUCH EASIER THAN IT LOOKS!

MATTHEW BAWERMAN

CONTENTS

ABOUT THE BOOK

SEVENTEEN YEARS AGO, when I first started a backyard flock — I had just two hens back then — if someone told me that I would write a book about how to manage a flock, I would've laughed.

But here we are! I started writing this book in July 2018, and after almost two years, it's ready. Consider this book a practical, easy-to-read guide for both beginners and experts that also includes helpful summaries and places where you can take notes at the end of each chapter.

GUIDED READING

For easier reading, I highlighted certain tips and information:

⭐ Mistakes I made in my own backyard homestead.

⭐ Life hacks I stumbled upon from my own experience.

⭐ Some historical information, just as useful context.

And throughout the book, you'll find footnotes to help you understand unfamiliar words or jargon.

This book is a compilation of my seventeen years of experience of raising chickens. I wrote this so you didn't have to undergo a similarly long path to find out all these tips. All you need is just a few hours with this book!

INTRODUCTION

P EOPLE HAVE BEEN raising poultry for several millennia. One of the most popular farm birds is chicken, although wild goose species were the first to be domesticated.

In modern poultry farming, chickens are the most popular birds — they make up about 80% of all farming poultry. Chickens are a source of valuable dietary meat and eggs, without which it is impossible today to imagine either American or European cuisine. In addition, chicken feathers have long been used in the economy.

This book contains comprehensive information for poultry farmers, both experienced and beginner. Here you will find useful information about the anatomical features of the bird, hen house building recommendations, maintenance and feeding, treatment and prevention of diseases, and descriptions of various types of feed. A separate chapter is devoted to breeding hens. At the end of the book are a few hacks I discovered over my seventeen years of experience as a poultry breeder, as well as tips on slaughtering and processing hens and preparing meat and eggs for storage.

8 TO 12

120

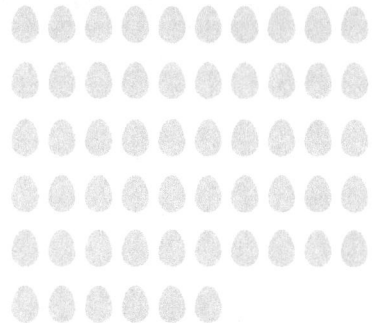

300

A bird's genetic potential achievement depends on the following:

⭐ Whether you meet the bird's need for air quality, temperature, and space;

⭐ The prevention, detection, and treatment of diseases;

⭐ Providing the right nutrients through a combination of proper feed, water, and tools;

⭐ How safe the birds are.

All these components are interdependent. Failure to comply with one of them will lead to a decrease in growth and productivity.

DID YOU KNOW? The exact time of chicken domestication isn't known, but it *is* known that the Red junglefowl are their ancestors. They live in Southeast Asia. In nature, this forest bird feeds on the seeds and fruits of trees, various insects, and earthworms.

Initially, the domestication of chickens was carried out exclusively for sporting purposes because of their fighting characteristics. It wasn't until much later that people began to keep tamed chickens. Eventually, they kept them specifically for egg production.

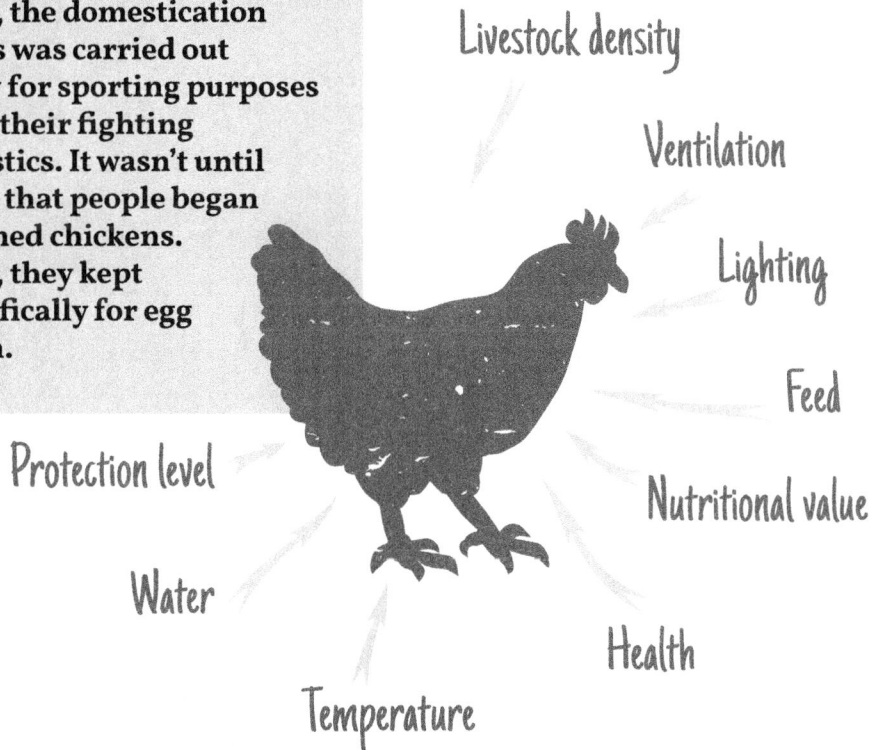

Livestock density

Ventilation

Lighting

Feed

Nutritional value

Protection level

Health

Water

Temperature

NOTES

PROS AND CONS OF KEEPING HENS

A BEGINNING POULTRY KEEPER needs to first decide on their goals. Do they intend to keep chickens for meat, eggs, or breeding and sales? Or do they simply want them as pets?

Keeping hens in the yard is convenient and profitable, especially if it's done correctly. You have to know the basics of keeping and feeding your feathered friends. And to be honest, it isn't very difficult.

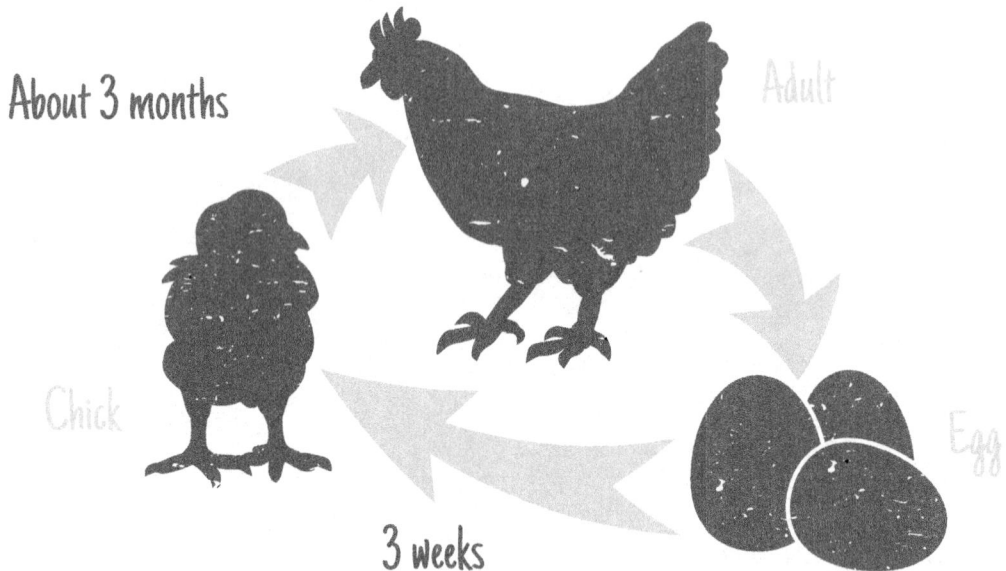

About 3 months

Adult

Chick

Egg

3 weeks

The main advantages of keeping hens:

✔ You get delicious, nutritious, and eco-friendly eggs and meat, all year round, great for both children and adults.

✔ You get fertilizer that can be used for agriculture.

✔ You can use their fluff and feathers to fill pillows and blankets.

✔ Chickens are low-cost and easy to keep. Adult hens in particular are low maintenance, so it won't be difficult for a beginner with the right approach.

✔ You can build a small henhouse with relative ease — there's no need for special equipment.

But with the good comes a little bad. Here are some of the disadvantages of keeping hens:

✘ Hens have a high mortality rate and are prone to diseases;

✘ You need to reserve a coop and a walking area for hens, which takes a little effort;

✘ You have to care for and clean the coop;

✘ You need to stay at home to feed and care for the birds daily.

CAUTION! A small flock may be kept without a walking area in the cages, but this can seriously affect their mental and physical health.

RECAP

★ Set up your backyard goals.

★ Raising hens has benefits and drawbacks. Weigh the pros and cons before deciding whether to start a flock.

NOTES

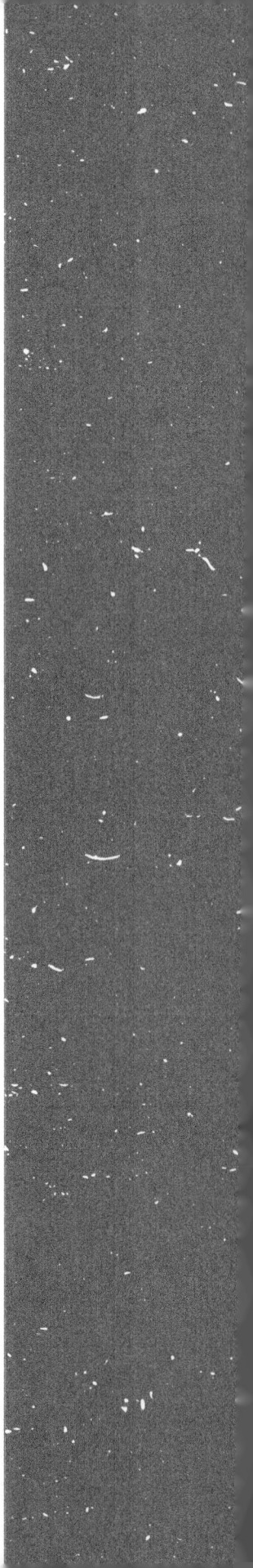

NOTES

WHICH BREED OF HEN SHOULD I CHOOSE?

TODAY THE NUMBER of hen breeds is vast. If you're going to get a flock, you need to choose a breed according to your goals.

For example, if you're raising hens only for meat or eggs, then it's recommended you find breeds specifically for those purposes.

Hens, like other poultry, are divided into several categories according to their appearance and strengths: decorative, sports, meat, egg, and meat/egg breeds. At farms and homesteads, hens are mainly used for meat, egg, or meat/egg production. Below are the most popular breeds for each category.

This chapter lists the most common breeds. If you want more examples, you'll find many more by doing a few simple Google searches.

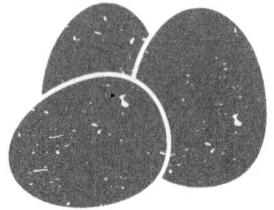

EGG LAYING BREEDS

The list of top performers:

AUSTRALORP
Brown Eggs ~ 200+ /year

Beginner Friendly	✔
Cold Hardy	✔
Dual Purpose	✔
Temperament	Docile

The Australian Orpington. An excellent egg layer that currently holds the world record for egg output in one year — 364! The Australorp is a dual purpose hen too. They dress out at a respectable 5–6lb and the meat is said to be good. The name "Australorp" derives from the types of chicken breeds used to formulate this excellent egg layer, which was Australian Black Orpingtons (Austral-orp). Developed in Australia in the early 1920's, and quickly adopted by the rest of the world, Australorps may be seen in

other countries as blue and white, but only the Black variety is recognized in the United States. A pleasure to have around, the temperament of the Australorp makes it a great chicken for the beginner. It is sweet, friendly, and docile to humans, and gets along easily with other hens and other animals. The Australorp was bred for egg production, and does not disappoint in that category. Typically a hen can lay well over 300 large brown eggs per year.

DELAWARE
Brown Eggs ~ 200+ /year

Beginner Friendly	✔
Cold Hardy	✔
Dual Purpose	✔
Temperament	Peaceful

These birds were all set to become the broiler bird of the US, and then the Cornish cross was introduced. The Delaware fell into near obscurity but has been making a comeback with the 'backyard crowd' of chicken keepers.

The Delaware is a respectable layer of 4 brown eggs per week. The hen is also a good dual purpose bird dressing out at 5lb.

The Delaware, once named Indian Rivers, was developed in the United States in the 1940's by a man named George Ellis. The fowl is a cross between a Plymouth Rock and a New Hampshire. Delaware as a breed was accepted into the American Poultry Association Standard of Perfection in 1952.

Owners report that the Delaware chicken is hardy, friendly, calm, and also funny to watch. Delawares are also good foragers. Hens mature rapidly and lay large brown or brown-tinted eggs that number 100 to 200+ per year, depending on certain conditions such as food supply and weather.

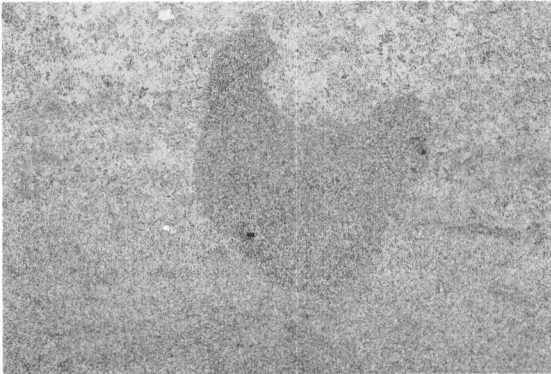

RHODE ISLAND RED
Brown Eggs ~ 200+ /year

Beginner Friendly	✔
Cold Hardy	✔
Dual Purpose	✔
Temperament	Confident

The Rhode Island Red is probably one of the most successful chicken breeds in the world!

It has spread from its homeland to all corners of the globe and is thriving even in the face of the modern industrial hens and intensive farming practices.

Why is it so successful?

They certainly are a bird that requires little in the way of care and are usually extremely healthy.

My personal opinion is because it is such a personable chicken — I have never met a Rhode Island hen that I didn't like!

NEW HAMPSHIRE
Brown Eggs ~ 200+ /year

Beginner Friendly	✔
Cold Hardy	✔
Dual Purpose	✔
Temperament	Peaceful

The New Hampshire chicken, named after its place of origin, the state of New Hampshire in the United States, is a relatively new breed; admitted to the Standard of Perfection by the American Poultry Association in 1935. They represent a specialized selection out of the Rhode Island Red breed. Deliberately selected for early feathering, fast growth, and maturity as well as large egg size and good meat conformation, certain strains were also noted for their vigor and hardiness.

BUCKEYE
Brown Eggs ~ 200+ /year

Beginner Friendly .... ✔

Cold Hardy .... ✔

Dual Purpose .... ✔

Temperament .... Peaceful

A dual purpose hen that thrives in the cold! The Buckeye chicken has the distinction of being the only breed to have been created by a woman.

Buckeyes will give you around 200 eggs each year. They can be butchered as young as 16 weeks and can dress out to a respectable 7–9lb bird.

The Buckeye is a breed originating in the late 19th century, in the U.S. state of Ohio. Around 1896, Nettie Metcalf, a resident of Warren, Ohio crossbred Barred Plymouth Rocks, Buff Cochins, and some black-breasted red games to produce the Buckeye.

They are very active, curious birds that love to be around people and other animals. They are also excellent hunters that will hunt for and catch mice. Their friendly curious nature makes them excellent pets as they have been known to jump into their humans' arms and poke their beaks in to find out what is going on.

Buckeyes lay about 200 medium sized brown eggs per year, and are very cold hardy; egg laying continues through the winter months.

PLYMOUTH ROCK
Brown Eggs ~ 200+ /year

Beginner Friendly	✔
Cold Hardy	✔
Dual Purpose	✖
Temperament	Peaceful

The Plymouth Rock breed got its start in Worcester, Massachusetts, USA in the 1860s. The first Plymouth Rock was Barred and other varieties developed later. All varieties of Plymouth Rock aside from the Barred and White varieties are relatively rare. The Plymouth Rock breed was recognized by the APA in 1874.

Some strains of this breed are good layers while others are bred principally for meat. Plymouth Rocks in general lay large size, medium brown color eggs, that number around 200–280 per year. A hardy bird even in cold weather, they tend to lay consistently all year long.

Generally, Plymouth Rocks are active, friendly with people, tame easily, and are not extremely aggressive with other chickens. Some males and hens are big and active enough, however to be quite a problem if they become aggressive.

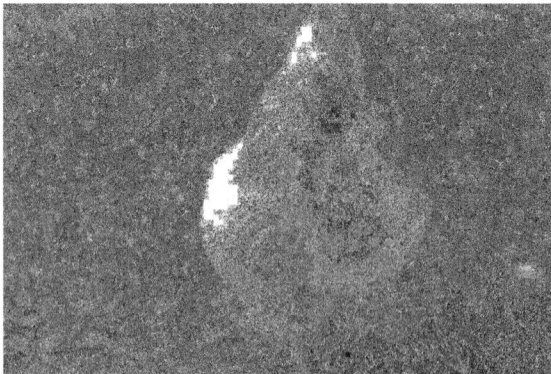

SUSSEX
Brown Eggs ~ 200+ /year

Beginner Friendly	✔
Cold Hardy	✔
Dual Purpose	✔
Temperament	Peaceful

The Sussex chicken has been well thought of in its' homeland of the UK for centuries now.

A good dependable layer in the region of 250–300 eggs per year. The speckled Sussex was the table fare of England until the newer, faster maturing breeds came along.

The Sussex breed of chicken has exactly the same history and temperament as the Speckled Sussex (above), but as one would expect, come in other colors aside from speckled.

Sussex chickens as a breed reached America about 1912 and was recognized by the American Poultry Association in three varieties: Speckled (1914), Red (1914), and Light (1929). In England another variety is recognized, the Brown. Not as popular, but still bred in the United States and Britain are additional colors, such as Coronation, Buff, White, and Silver.

Most Sussex are steady egg layers, again tend to lay large light brown eggs, 200–350 per year.

BROWN LEGHORN
White Eggs ~ 200 /year

Beginner Friendly	✔
Cold Hardy	✘
Dual Purpose	✘
Temperament	Confident

The Brown Leghorn is a useful dual-purpose bird. It will lay an average of 280 eggs per year.

They can be butchered at 16 weeks and weigh a good 5–6lb. They are also good foragers, so the feed ratio is good.

Although Leghorns are not usually known for their meat qualities, the meat is said to be decent on the brown variety.

If you're interested in reading more about egg laying breeds, make sure to read 10 Breeds of Chicken That Will Lay Lots of Eggs for You.

The Brown Leghorn Chicken is one variety of the Leghorns that originated in Tuscany, Italy in the early 1800's. They were initially called "Italians", then "Livorno", which is the name of the port city in Italy where they were exported from, but by 1865 were knows as Leghorn, which is simply Anglican for the Italian word Livorno. Leghorns were exported to America in the mid 1800's, and although the Leghorn breed itself originated in Italy, most of the color varieties (developed possibly for better camouflage) including the Brown Leghorn were developed in Great Britain, America and Denmark.

Leghorns tend to be skittish and flighty birds, nervous birds. They're not very interested in mingling with people and mostly like to be left alone. Combined with the fact that Leghorns are incredibly fast runners, very difficult to catch, they might not be the best breed to be recommended as pets.

Leghorns, brown as well as white, are prolific egg layers. A good hen will lay in the vicinity of 300 large, white eggs a year.

WHITE LEGHORN
White Eggs ~ 200 /year

Beginner Friendly	✔
Cold Hardy	✔
Dual Purpose	✖
Temperament	Confident

The White Leghorn Chicken is one variety of the Leghorns that originated in Tuscany, Italy and exported to America in 1928. They were initially called "Italians", then "Livorno", which is the name of the port city in Italy where they were exported from, but by 1865 were knows as Leghorn, which is simply English for the Italian word Livorno.

Leghorn chickens are known to be amazingly active, sometimes nervous or flighty, hard working foragers that often have little time for humans. That said, they can also be quite friendly backyard chickens if handled early from chicks. Because of their tendency to work at scratching and foraging for their meals, the feed bill for Leghorns will usually be lower than other breeds.

To boot, White Leghorns can be known to lay upwards of 300 large white eggs per year, all year long, also making them a favorite with commercial egg producers.

MEAT BREEDS

If your looking for a great meat breed here are top 3 picks:

CORNISH
Light Brown Eggs ~ 100 /year

Beginner Friendly	✘
Cold Hardy	✔
Dual Purpose	✘
Temperament	Confident

The fluffy hen that loves to be cuddled and can easily become a lap chicken. This bird would be suitable as a therapy bird.

Cornish chickens originated from Cornwall County in England, and a heritage breed, a best guess for development was around 1820. They were introduced to America and became part of the APA Standard chicken in 1893. Intended initially as an all purpose breed, their heavy body and muscular nature quickly gave rise to overwhelmingly meat-only chicken. Most domestic chicken used in the meat industry today are at least part Cornish chicken.

Cornish temperament tends to be aggressive, loud, and active, and are not usually recommended for the backyard chicken keeper.

They are the quintessential meat chicken. They grow fast, too fast for their bodies to keep up; hence they must be butchered to save them from suffering.

They are ready to cull at 4–6 weeks and by this age will weigh around 8lb. The downside to this bird is their feed consumption which is high, making them not so great in the feed ratio.

Given the fact that these hens are most used as a meat breed, you would not expect them to be the best egg layers. Cornish typically lay about 100–120 medium light brown eggs per year.

BRESSE
Brown Eggs ~ 200 /year

Beginner Friendly	✖
Cold Hardy	✖
Dual Purpose	✔
Temperament	Flighty

About 500 years ago, Bresse emerged as a distinct chicken breed. Technically, the birds of this breed must be raised within the legally defined area of the historic region of Bresse, between the Rhone River and the French Alps. Bresse Chickens are considered the best tasting, most expensive chickens in the world. To maintain the strictest quality standards, the raising and selling of Bresse chickens is rigidly controlled by the French government. There are rules about how much land they must have access to, what they must be fed, and how they must be processed. The French argue that for a Bresse to be called a Bresse it must have been raised in France.

The original Bresse line of chickens is still alive and well, living in France. The French Bresse hen is a breed apart. They are cared for and fed a special diet, all of which is monitored by the French Agriculture Department. All this attention makes for a costly chicken dinner.

For this reason, American breeders of this chicken call them "American Bresse". First brought into the US from France in 2011, American breeders have since tried to approximate the traditional methods of raising Bresse by providing them access to rich pasture and finishing them on organic grains and dairy products.

If one were to inclined to try and raise Bresse chickens, you could expect Bresse chickens to have peaceful temperaments and be pleasant barnyard companions. They lay about 250 large, golden brown eggs per year.

There are now American Bresse chickens. They are essentially much the same bird but raised differently.

The meat is said to be superb tasting. They are culled at 16–20 weeks and will dress out at 5–7 lb. They are slower growers so feed conversion is average.

JERSEY GIANT
Brown Eggs ~ 200 /year

Beginner Friendly .... ✔

Cold Hardy .... ✔

Dual Purpose .... ✔

Temperament .... Peaceful

The Jersey Giant chicken is the largest purebred breed of chicken. The result of a breeding program that began around 1870 by John and Thomas Black of New Jersey, the original objective of the breed was as a replacement for the turkey. The resulting adult birds are massive in size with mature roosters weighing in at 13 lbs, and hens up to 10 lbs.

They are slow growers and can start to be culled around 16 weeks.

Originally bred to be both a commercial meat and egg chicken, the Jersey Giant breed is not used for commercial farming because it takes 6 months for them to grow to full size, as opposed to 2 months for other breeds.

The Black Jersey Giant was added to the Standard of Perfection of the American Poultry Association in 1922. The White variety was added in 1947, and Blue in 2002.

The Jersey Giant is known as a calm and docile breed with an even temperament. Aside from the fact that they will consume more food in a lifetime than a smaller breed, and need more space, they would make good backyard chickens.

A Jersey Giant hen lays 150–200 very large, light to medium brown eggs per year.

FRIENDLY BREEDS

For many people, it is important that their flock interacts with them. A flock than runs away when they see you or just plain ignores you is not a pleasurable thing.

Some breeds just love people and enjoy being divas when their humans are around, others could not care less, and worse yet, some wish you would just go away.

A shortlist of some of the friendliest and most interactive birds we know, including those that we think would make great therapy/service pets.

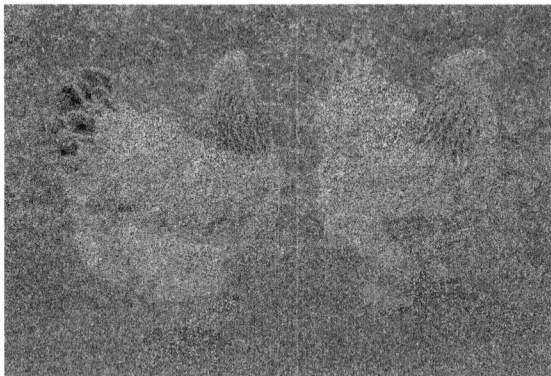

BRAHMA
Brown Eggs ~ 150 /year

Beginner Friendly	✖
Cold Hardy	✔
Dual Purpose	✔
Temperament	Friendly

They are large cuddly hens. They can be shy, but are usually friendly and enjoy human company.

The ancestry of the Brahma traces back to development in America from very large fowl imported between 1850 and 1890 from China after older breeding from Chittigong fowl in India. "Brahma" derives from the name of the Brahmaputra River, which flows through both China and India. They were developed into three color varieties — the Light, the Dark, and the Buff.

With respect to temperament, Brahmas are very friendly, as long as you've raised them to enjoy the company of people. They are quiet, docile, and calm birds who get along great with other chickens, and enjoy taking treats from your hand.

Considered a superior winter-layer, they produce the bulk of their eggs from October to May, and number around 150 per year. The eggs of the Brahma are large and uniformly medium brown in color.

COCHIN
Brown Eggs ~ 100 /year

Beginner Friendly .... ✔

Cold Hardy .... ✔

Dual Purpose .... ✖

Temperament .... Friendly

Cochin first originated in ancient China, and have also been known as "Shanghai" birds or "Cochin-Chinas". Introduced to the West in the mid-1800's, they were partly responsible for the upsurge in popularity of keeping chickens that was called "hen fever" in Britain and the US. Known as one of the ornamental breeds, cochins are bred in several color patterns: Buff, Partridge, White, Black, Silver Laced, Golden Laced, Blue, Brown, and Barred.

Cochins are known to be quite peaceful and calm, easy to handle, and friendly, but are prone to broodiness, so are not known for egg production. They average about 160 large brown eggs per year.

FAVEROLLE
Light Brown Eggs ~ 200 /year

Beginner Friendly .... ✔

Cold Hardy .... ✔

Dual Purpose .... ✔

Temperament .... Friendly

These Faverolles chickens will make you smile. They are talkative, curious, friendly and a bit scatter brained!

ORPINGTON
Brown Eggs ~ 200 /year

Beginner Friendly .... ✔

Cold Hardy .... ✔

Dual Purpose .... ✔

Temperament .... Friendly

The Orpington chicken is a very calm and friendly bird. Never in a hurry to go anywhere, curious and will be your friend for life if you give her treats.

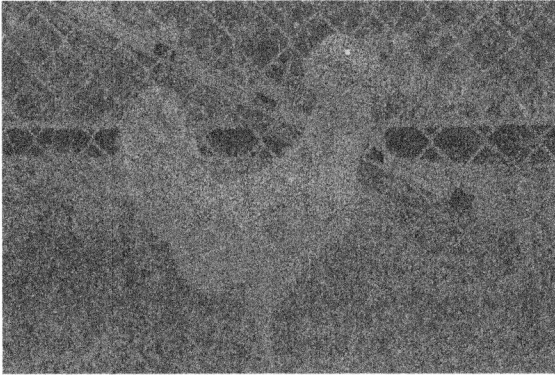

POLISH
White Eggs ~ 150 /year

Beginner Friendly	✔
Cold Hardy	✔
Dual Purpose	✖
Temperament	Friendly

The Polish hen is unmistakable with the pom-pom on the head. The pom-pom can get in the way of their vision at times, so may need light trimming.

When you see a Polish chicken a smile is pretty much guaranteed.

The Polish origins are not known, yet there have been paintings of them dating back to the 1600's. Some historians believe they originated from Spain and were then transported to Holland. It's thought the Polish breed made its way to the US in the early 1800's. The name of the breed relates not to Poland, but to the Polish military hats with a feather crest. Bearded and non-bearded types of White, Silver, Golden, Buff Laced, and Black are some color varieties of Polish chicken breed recognized by the American Poultry Association as early as 1874.

The Polish is mainly an ornamental bird, but was once used for egg production before the Leghorn became popular. These birds are very prolific, laying around 200 or more medium white eggs per year.

Polish chicken is very easy to handle and tame. They are similar to Leghorn chicken in both size and type. They are also good as pets, however not the best for the beginner chicken farmer. Their beautiful top crest must be frequently checked for dirt and wetness, as this can cause ongoing eye infections if left untreated.

RECAP

Name	Photo	Eggs/year	Beginner Friendly	Cold Hardy	Dual Purpose	Temperament
EGG LAYING BREEDS						
Australorp		200+	✔	✔	✔	Docile
Delaware		200+	✔	✔	✔	Peaceful
Rhode Island Red		200+	✔	✔	✔	Confident
New Hampshire		200+	✔	✔	✔	Peaceful
Buckeye		200+	✔	✔	✔	Peaceful
Plymouth Rock		200+	✔	✔	✘	Peaceful
Sussex		200+	✔	✔	✔	Peaceful
Brown Leghorn		200	✔	✘	✘	Confident
White Leghorn		200	✔	✔	✘	Confident

Name	Photo	Eggs/year	Beginner Friendly	Cold Hardy	Dual Purpose	Temperament
MEAT BREEDS						
Cornish		100	✘	✔	✘	Confident
Bresse		200	✘	✘	✔	Flighty
Jersey Giant		200	✔	✔	✔	Peaceful
FRIENDLY BREEDS						
Brahma		150	✘	✔	✔	Friendly
Cochin		100	✔	✔	✘	Friendly
Faverolle		200	✔	✔	✔	Friendly
Orpington		200	✔	✔	✔	Friendly
Polish		150	✔	✔	✘	Friendly

NOTES

ON BUYING HENS AND CHICKS

ONCE YOU'VE WEIGHED the pros and cons of keeping hens, found a suitable breed, and definitely decided to get a flock, then your next step will be to buy chickens. Whether you buy baby chicks and raise them yourself or choose to buy adult hens that are ready to lay will depend on a few factors.

BUYING CHICKS OR CHICKENS

Most people tend to buy baby chicks over fully grown chickens because it's cheaper. Plus, raising babies is more of an enjoyable experience — baby chicks are some of the cutest creatures on the planet.

The downside is that raising chicks is extra work. So make sure you're up to the challenge.

VS

BUYING BABY CHICKS

PROS

✔ The enjoyment of raising young chicks into fully grown chickens;

✔ You can socialize them so that they are family friendly;

✔ It's cheaper than buying chickens;

✔ You can order online and have them delivered easily;

✔ You can choose your favorite breed and mix and match from hatcheries;

✔ You can raise healthy chickens by feeding them and caring for them that lay healthy eggs.

CONS

✘ It's more work, especially in the first eight weeks — they need to be cared for and nurtured;

✘ You need to make a brooder or an area to raise them;

✘ Up to six months may pass before you see any eggs;

✘ You might accidentally get roosters if you order from hatcheries.

BUYING GROWN CHICKEN

PROS

- ✔ Chickens will be ready to lay eggs soon after you get them, or immediately, depending on how old they are;

- ✔ It's more hands-off, as you don't need to nurture or raise them;

- ✔ There's no chance you'll get a rooster. if you know what you're doing (I'll explain shortly how to tell a rooster from a hen below).

CONS

- ✖ You have to physically go and buy them. You can't order chickens online.

- ✖ If they weren't brought up correctly, they may be anti-social and unfriendly.

- ✖ You may not be able to choose certain breeds based on your location.

- ✖ It's hard to tell how old the chickens really are (I'll explain you to do it in a bit).

- ✖ There's a chance of buying a "lemon" and being taken advantage of by sellers.

SO, WHAT'S RIGHT FOR YOU?

- ★ **Go for baby chicks** if you have a little spare time to care for and raise them. If you have children, you'll be able to socialize the chickens with your kids. They may even become beloved family pets.

- ★ **Go for fully grown chickens** if you're just in it for the eggs and aren't interested in raising and nurturing young chicks.

WHERE TO BUY

When it comes to buying chicks, you have three options, generally:

★ Buy online from a hatchery and have them delivered;

★ Buy from a local feed store or hatchery;

★ Buy from a local seller after finding them on a buy/sell classified, such as Craigslist.

Buying online from a hatchery is the most popular option. It's cheap, quick, and easy, and you can generally pick and choose a few different breeds of chicken, rather than buying whatever is available locally.

The only problem with hatcheries is that most of them require minimum orders of fifteen or more chicks, meaning urban chicken owners struggle to find somewhere that will only sell them a few chicks.

If a hatchery isn't your thing, a local feed store can help you out. Simply call them up and order your chicks when spring comes around.

Finally, online classifieds can provide a great way to find local breeders in your area.

Be aware, though, that when buying chicks in this manner, they will most often not be vaccinated. However, you can take them to your local hatchery to get vaccinated.

TRAPS TO AVOID

When buying chickens, it's important to do your due diligence and ask the seller the right questions (especially if buying them privately). Otherwise, you may end up with a lemon!

Remember that anyone who raises or breeds chickens will more likely get rid of unproductive or less desirable birds over the better performing birds — and most of the time, this means selling them to a clueless, first-time chicken owner.

In particular, you need to watch out for:

★ Buying an unhealthy hen;

★ Buying a hen that's past its "use-by date" and won't lay as many eggs;

★ Ending up with a rooster after you thought you were buying a young hen.

35

AVOID BUYING AN UNHEALTHY HEN

A hen with health complications will be more trouble than it's worth, as it could provide less eggs or even spread the sickness to your other chicken.

Be sure to also look out for the following warning signs:

★ A discolored and blemished comb (it should be a nice solid red or pink if they are young);

★ Flaky legs (they should be smooth);

★ An unclean bottom/vent (it should be clean, which indicates that it has not been laying already);

★ Dull eyes and a dirty nose and beak (eyes should be bright and clean, as should the nose and beak).

LIFE HACK ALERT! Here's how you avoid this: pick up every chicken you're considering and hold it in your arms. Notice how it reacts. Is it aggressive? Does it seem like it's in pain?

AVOID BUYING A HEN THAT HAS PAST ITS "POINT OF LAY"

The "point of lay" is the time when a chicken starts laying eggs. The closer to this time the better, as chickens lay most of their eggs in the first few years; after that, their laying steadily declines.

There are a big list of factors that will influence the age a hen starts laying. However, in general, if you're being sold a chicken at the "point of lay," it should be between sixteen and eighteen weeks old. (Chickens generally start laying at six months of age.)

It's important that you don't get sold a chicken that is actually well past its point of lay. Otherwise, you may end up with a chicken that's passed its "use-by date," meaning they won't provide you with as many eggs.

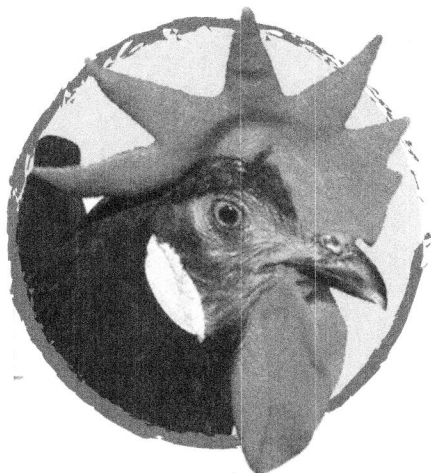

Bright = Young hen. Ready to lay

Dull = Older hen. Past the point of lay

How to tell if your chicken is really at the point of lay:

★ The comb should be relatively small, and the wattle and comb should just be starting to turn pink.

★ The feathers at the rear (called the vent) should be clean. If they are not, this is an indication that the hen has already been laying eggs.

★ Ask the seller exactly how old the chicken is and wait for their reaction. They should have a good idea and respond with something like "eighteen weeks." If they say "umm" and "ahh" and give you a vague answer, like "a little over a year old," be suspicious. Be very suspicious.

COMB
BEAK
COMB
WATTLE
WATTLE
HACKLES
CAPE
CAPE
TAIL
WING
WING
SADDLE
TAIL
VENT
BREAST
THIGH
FLUFF
SHANK
SICKLES
SPURS

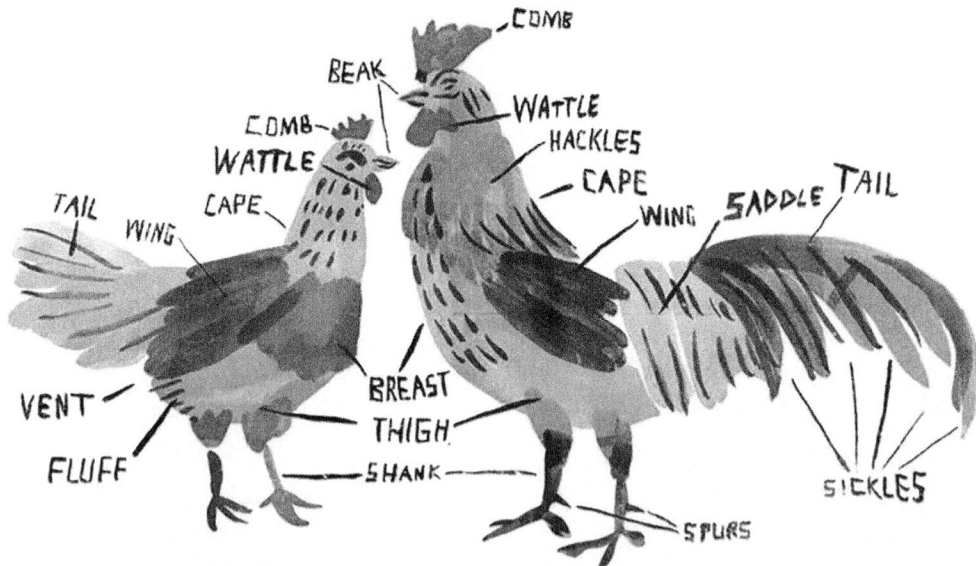

HOW TO TELL A ROOSTER FROM A HEN

It's not easy for first-time chicken owners to tell the difference between a young hen and a young rooster. But with practice, you'll improve. The first step is to look at the bird for clues.

FEATHERS

Roosters often have a distinguishing hackle or neck feathers and saddle or back feathers. In roosters, these feathers are often pointed, whereas on hens, these feathers are rounded. If there is more than one rooster in the group, they will often square off, and their hackle feathers will puff out as they stare at each other. Rooster tail feathers have a curve to them. Because of their shape, they are often called "sickle feathers."

LEGS

Roosters often have thicker legs than hens. They also have pointed spurs — sharp, bone-like growths just above the toes on the rooster's leg — which hens usually don't have. Roosters use these spurs to protect the flock and defend themselves. Old hens will sometimes have spurs, but they will not be as long or as sharp as those on roosters.

WATTLES AND COMBS

Roosters usually have tall, upright combs that are larger than hens' combs. If the rooster is young, he will have a more pronounced comb than female chicks of the same age. Roosters tend to have redder combs and wattles at an earlier age than chicks of the same age. When mature, rooster wattles are very large compared to hen wattles.

COLORING

Roosters often have "showier" plumage than hens. Their colors are often bright and vibrant. Many roosters have iridescent feathers that capture light and reflect beautiful blue and green highlights. If the bird has iridescent plumage, it is most likely a rooster.

RECAP

★ Check the Pros and Cons of buying chicks over chickens. Make a choice that's more suitable for you.

★ Go for baby chicks if you have a little spare time to care for and raise them, and if you'd like a family pet.

★ Go for fully grown chickens if you're just in it for the eggs.

★ There are at least ways you can buy a flock:

☆ Online from a hatchery (delivery often available);

☆ In person at a local feed store or hatchery;

☆ From a local seller that you find in the buy/sell classifieds, perhaps on Craigslist.

★ You need to watch out for:

☆ Unhealthy hens;

☆ Hens that are past their "use-by date," which won't lay as many eggs;

☆ Ending up with a rooster when you thought you were buying a hen! Examine the feathers, legs, wattles and combs, and coloring for clues.

NOTES

HOUSING HENS

GENERAL
GUIDELINES

THE IMPORTANCE OF following general guidelines for working with poultry to ensure their well-being — for maximal productivity and profitability — cannot be over-estimated. A person who understands how to care for a bird can spot a problem in their herd and fix it quickly.

When caring for birds, you should apply the recommendations in this book and use them along with your professional experience, knowledge, and understanding of your herd's characteristics.

Effective work with poultry is the result of close human interaction with the flock. You should know the birds well enough to be able to "feel" the birds and the "microclimate" of their house. To be able to do this, you need to closely monitor the behavior of the birds and the coop conditions. This type of observation is often called "feel the flock" and is an ongoing process that uses all the senses.

The microclimate in the house and the behavior of the birds should be observed a few times a day. It's important to enter the coop periodically in order to observe the herd.

At the entrance of the coop, knock gently and then open the door slowly.

You should slowly enter the henhouse and stop upon entering, so that the birds have time to get used to your presence. At this time, it is necessary to use all the senses in order to assess the situation in the henhouse: **VISION, HEARING, SENSE OF SMELL, and TOUCH.**

Vision

Hearing

Sense of smell

Taste

Touch

VISION:

★ **Bird distribution.** If there are areas that the birds avoid, this may indicate a microclimate problem (draft, cold, light, etc.).

★ **Breathing patterns.** Are the birds breathing heavily? Panting observed in a specific area of the house may indicate a problem with air movement or temperature.

★ **Behavior.** What's their feed and consumption like? Are they resting?

★ **Litter* condition.** Are there any spots of wet letter in the coop, caused by water leaks from the drinkers or excess moisture?

★ **Feeders and drinkers.** Are they installed at the correct height? Is there food in the feeders? Are the drinkers leaking?

* Litter is a poultry housing flooring, based on the repeated spreading of straw or sawdust material.

HEARING:

★ **Flock sounds.** Do the birds sneeze? Cough? Show signs of difficulty breathing? What sound does the flock make? What sounds do the birds make compared to your previous visit? Might any of these changes be attributed to the coop's dusty-ness?

LIFE HACK ALERT!
The evening is the best time for this type of observation, as there will be less external noise.

TOUCH:

★ **Air quality.** How does the air feel? Stuffy (wet), cold, hot? A lot, a little, or no air movement? These qualities may indicate specific microclimate problems, like, for example, insufficient ventilation.

★ **Feed quality.** How much dust is in the grains? Are the granules strong? Do the granules easily break in the hand or the feeder?

★ **Litter quality.** Touch a piece of litter. If the litter collects in a lump after being compressed in your hand (in other words, if it doesn't crumble), this means there's excess moisture in the litter, which may indicate poor ventilation (see more in the "How to Build a Coop -> Equipment and materials for hens flock -> Litter" section).

SENSE OF SMELL:

★ **Feed.** How does it smell? Is the smell fresh or musty?

★ **Microclimate.** What's the smell in the coop like? Can you smell ammonia?

After entering the coop and observing the flock and microclimate, slowly walk around the entire length of the henhouse, making observations according to what you detect through your senses. At the same time, it is very important for you to go around the entire house to make sure that there are no significant microclimate fluctuations or concerning issues with the birds' behavior. And don't just observe from the point where you're standing. Squat down and pick up any birds that aren't running away from you. **Do these birds look sick?** See how the bird moves in front of you and behind your back. Does the bird get back to the empty space created by your movement? You should stop periodically to catch an individual bird and inspect it, making sure that:

★ **The eyes** are clean and free from signs of irritation.

★ **The skin** doesn't have pigmentation, scratches, or surface hock* damage.

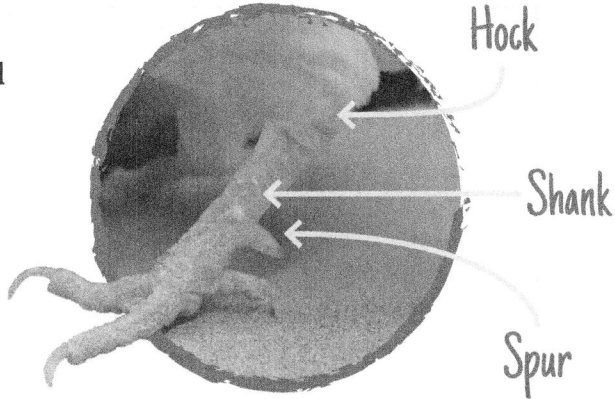

Hock

Shank

Spur

★ **The pectoral** muscle is clean without damage.

★ **The plumage** is clean and smooth.

★ **The bird's gait** seems healthy.

★ **The pads on their feet and hock** are clean and free from signs of irritation.

★ **The cloaca**** is clean and free from liquid droppings.

★ **The beak and tongue** have no discharge from the nasopharynx, there's no food adhered to the beak, and the tongue isn't discolored.

★ **The goiter** doesn't contain particles of litter, and the goiter is soft, not hard. (A soft goiter indicates water availability.)

★ **General behavior, posture, and movement seem healthy.**

---

* The hock is the joint between the drumstick on a chicken and the 'ankle' joint.
** The cloaca is the single posterior opening for a bird's digestive, urinary, and reproductive tracts and is used to expel feces and lay eggs.

These observations will give you a near complete snapshot of the health of your flock or coop.

LIFE HACK ALERT!
But keep in mind: there are no two identical flocks or coops. Each household or farm is unique!

If we only deal with reviewing notes (growth, feed intake, etc.), we can miss important signals from the birds, which might be a sign that something is wrong with the microclimate. Using all the senses, you will get a general idea of the microclimate and the state of the flock, and you'll also understand what the signs of normal herd behavior are for your flock. That's important to know, because it gives you the ability to notice violations of the norm and immediately fix any problems.

Feed Conversion Ratio (FCR) at each specific age is the same for the whole population; however, each herd has its own needs. To understand the individual requirements of the herd and to be able to respond to these requirements, you need to know and feel what's normal for your flock.

Your experience "communicating" with the birds, how you sense the flock is doing, and your knowledge and skills in matters of keeping the livestock will not only provide the "five freedoms of animal welfare" to your hens (see below) but also help to improve the flock. It's like icing on the cake!

FIVE FREEDOMS OF ANIMAL WELFARE

1. **Freedom from hunger and thirst** by easy access to fresh water and a diet that helps animals maintain full health and vigor;

2. **Freedom from discomfort** by an appropriate environment that includes shelter and a comfortable resting area;

3. **Freedom from pain, injury, or disease** by prevention through rapid diagnosis and treatment.

CAUTION! It's important to keep a weekly or daily record of indicators such as height, weight, feed intake, water, number of eggs laid, etc. in order to respond to problems in a timely manner and quickly find the cause.

4. **Freedom to express normal behavior** by providing sufficient space, proper facilities, and company of the animal's own kind;

5. **Freedom from fear and distress** by providing conditions that avoid suffering.

RECAP

★ It is necessary to use all the senses in order to assess the situation in the henhouse: **VISION, HEARING, SENSE OF SMELL,** and **TOUCH.**

★ Periodically inspect each bird for issues with the eyes, skin, pectoral muscle, plumage, gait health, feet and hock pads, cloaca, beak, tongue, goiter, and general behaviors.

★ Remember the five freedoms of animal welfare:

☆ Freedom from hunger and thirst;

☆ Freedom from discomfort;

☆ Freedom from pain, injury, or disease;

☆ Freedom to express normal behavior;

☆ Freedom from fear and distress.

NOTES

FEED AND WATER

T IS VERY important that your flock is provided with the necessary set of nutrients using an effective feeding program for broilers or laying hens in order to optimize productivity. Feeding and watering systems affect the level of feed and water consumption, as well as the compliance of the selected feeding program with the flock needs.

Food is one of the main costs. To ensure optimal performance, diets should be designed to provide the bird with a balanced ratio of metabolic energy, protein, amino acids, minerals, vitamins, and fatty acids. The choice of feeding program will depend on your goals and, in particular, on what the main focus of your household farm is: meat production or for eggs.

LIFE HACK ALERT! By the way, bread residue soaked in water can make up to 50% of the bird's diet.

TYPES OF FEED AND THEIR PROPERTIES

The raw materials used for a chicken's diet should be fresh and high quality, both in terms of digestibility and physical structure.

Excess grain from your kitchen can be used as feed on a household farm, including potato peelings and pieces of black and white bread. (Just make sure the bread isn't moldy.)

In addition, free-range hens can find additional feed by themselves.

To feed the birds in the winter, prepare fodder in advance using vitamin hay, needles, and silage.

Fodder conservation allows you to save money on expensive concentrated feed, which is important in a homestead economy.

Feed should consist of organic substances, minerals, and water. Organic substances include protein, carbohydrates, fats, and vitamins. Conventionally, the feed used for feeding chickens can be divided into four groups according to their composition: protein, carbohydrate, vitamin, and mineral.

LIFE HACK ALERT! Bread leftovers and potato peelings can also be specially prepared for winter feed. Mash the residue into a thin layer and place it on a baking sheet. Then transfer this to the oven. Cook over low heat for about 30 minutes. When finished, the residue will turn into brittle. Store in a dry place inside a canvas bag.

PROTEIN FEED

Protein is an integral part of a living organism's cells. The birds' need for protein during their laying period is high because protein is necessary for the formation of protein in the eggs.

With a protein deficiency in the diet, the hen's development is delayed, their growth slows down, the eggshell formation is disturbed, the plumage is stiff and brittle, spermatogenesis* slows down, and so on.

Protein feed can be of plant or animal origin.

Protein feeds of animal origin are most valuable, as they are rich not only in high-grade protein but also in B vitamins and minerals.

----

* Spermatogenesis, the origin and development of the sperm cells within the rooster's reproductive organs.

★ **Dairy products.** It's recommended to introduce into the poultry diet, periodically, feed that's prepared with milk powder. Milk powder contains easily digestible nutrients for chicks and chickens: 30–33% protein, 0.5–1.5% fat, 44–47% milk sugar, 7–8% ash elements, 5–7% water. For young hens and chicks, milk powder should be given in an amount of 3% of the dry portion of the diet.

★ **Fish or fishmeal.** For feeding hens, usually, only small fish unsuitable for human consumption should be used. Before feeding the hens, boil and crush the fish. It is necessary, periodically, to include fishmeal into a chicken's diet, as it's one of the most nutritious protein feeds.

★ **Meat and bone meal.** Meat and bone meal come from the waste of meat processing plants. In nutritional value, this product is slightly inferior to fishmeal. Meat and bone meal are rich in lysine but poor in other amino acids. The meat and bone meal composition also includes fat (11%), ash elements (up to 30%), and A and E vitamins.

★ **Chicken egg.** This is one of the most nutritionally complete animal feeds. In addition to protein, it contains a lot of vitamins and mineral salts. Chicken egg is an indispensable food for chicks. For adult hens, a boiled chicken egg should be included in the diet during the laying period, as well as during molting.

★ **Earthworms.** A useful treat for poultry is earthworms, which can be specially grown on a personal plot.

★ **Fly larvae.** You can use maggots to feed chicks. Breeding flies is really easy, and under favorable conditions, you can get enough of them in less than a week.

★ **Crankbait.** Mosquito larvae are well known to anglers and aquarium fish lovers.

★ **June bugs.** For hen feeding, June bugs are used in dried and crushed form. They can be added as powder to soft feeds.

★ **Soy.** In terms of the ratio of essential amino acids, soy protein is closest to animal feed protein. Soy in heat-treated grain form can be introduced into the diet of poultry as up to 80% of the total weight of the grain mixture.

★ **Peas.** Peas contain all the essential amino acids necessary for a normal chicken's body development. In feed, it is used in a crushed and ground form. Peas are included can be included in the diet of chickens as 10% of a dry mixture.

★ **Wheat bran.** Wheat bran can be used as feed for chicks and adult birds not exceeding 5–7% of the weight of dry feed.

CARBOHYDRATE FEED

Carbohydrate feeds aren't just readily eaten by chickens — they're excellent for muscle and organs function and help chickens keep a normal body temperature.

Conventionally, carbohydrate feed is divided into grain and succulent.

Cereal feeds are the main source of energy. They make up at least 55% of the poultry diet. In addition, in whole and in crushed form, they are easily digested, readily eaten by hens, and are the basis for high-calorie nutrition.

Cereal grains consist of starch (70%), protein (8–12%), fat (2–8%), and minerals (1.5–4%). However, cereal protein lacks such essential amino acids as lysine and methionine, and barley, oats, and millet contain a large amount of fiber that is poorly absorbed by the bird.

★ **Corn.** This is one of the most valuable cereal feeds since it contains a very small amount of fiber (no more than 2.5%), which is six times less than oats. And in terms of protein, corn is a leader among cereals. Corn contains carotene (in 1 kg of yellow corn, up to 20 mcg). However, for proper nutrition, corn is not enough, since its protein content is very low — only about 10%. It does not make up for the poultry's need for minerals and B vitamins.

LIFE HACK ALERT! The nutritional value of oats can be increased by germinating before feeding.

★ **Oats.** To feed the hens oats, all film from the grains must be removed. For young chickens, oats must be minced. Oat meal must be sieved. The fiber in large quantities isn't digestible for the birds; it causes a blockage of the gastrointestinal tract and leads to a young chicken's death. Therefore, oat meal should not comprise more than 20% of a chicken's diet.

★ **Wheat.** Wheat feed is often used for poultry. It is rich in B and E vitamins. Wheat is protein-rich, although it is slightly inferior to corn in nutritional value. It is included in the diet of hens of all breeds and of any age. For feeding young chickens, wheat should be in a ground form but comprise no more than 30% of the whole diet.

★ **Rye.** This grain is rarely used as feed. It is especially undesirable to include freshly harvested rye in a chicken's diet, as the grain contains mucus, which causes digestive upset in hens. For the same reason, they shouldn't be included in the diet of young chickens. In exceptional cases, for poultry older than 30 days of age, rye can be given in whole meal form not exceeding 10% of an all-grain feed.

★ **Barley.** This feed is given to a flock without shells, to reduce fiber content. Young chickens can be fed coarsely ground, sifted barley as part of a grain-flour mixture (no more than 40% of the diet).

CAUTION! Waste from sorting and processing grain in large farms should be used with great care, as they may contain toxins (weed seeds, ergot, etc.). By the way, the nutritional value of this waste is low.

★ **Millet.** This is a valuable poultry feed, especially for young chickens. Hens are fed without shells, and for young chickens, it's given in ground form. Millet, especially yellow millet, is carotene-rich. But as a feed for poultry, it is used infrequently because of its high nutritional value for humans.

★ **Potato.** It contains all the nutrition that hens need. Before feeding, peel the potatoes, boil them in slightly salted water, and mix with grated carrots and 2–3 drops of cooking oil. If the mixture turns out too wet and sticky, you can add semolina.

★ **Carrot.** Fresh carrots are good for hens of all ages, at 5–30 grams per bird. Before feeding the birds, coarsely grate carrots then mix with breadcrumbs, semolina, and an oily solution of A, D, and E vitamins.

★ **Turnip.** These are significantly inferior to carrots and beets in terms of vitamins and minerals, but many poultry farmers include them in the hen's diet.

★ **Pumpkin.** This is a cheap and affordable feed. It consists of sugar, carotene, and vitamin B2. It can be used in a mashed or crushed form and comprise up to 15% of a diet. Do not use for feeding chicks under five days of age!

★ **Cabbage.** This contains proteins, minerals, and vitamins. Both whole and chopped cabbage can be fed to poultry.

LIFE HACK ALERT! In the coop, where hens are kept, you can hang a whole cabbage on a rope so that they can feed themselves.

FATS

Fats, which are part of the cells, are used to generate thermal and mechanical energy. By origin, they are divided into animal and plant fats. Whey, meat, and fish meal contain animal fats. Corn and soy are rich in vegetable fats. The poultry's body also synthesizes fat from carbohydrates and proteins, so the feed should be balanced. This will prevent hens from becoming obese, so they can stay productive.

VITAMIN FEED

Vitamins are organic substances that have a complex chemical structure. They have a great influence on the vital processes of a living organism. The absence of vitamins in a poultry's diet causes vitamin deficiency or hypovitaminosis, which affects metabolism, health, and productivity.

Currently, more than two dozen vitamins are known. They are divided into fat-soluble (A, D, E, K) and water-soluble (C and B vitamins) vitamins.

★ **Vitamin A, or Retinol.** This vitamin is mainly found in foods of animal origin, such as milk, eggs, fish liver, etc. Provitamin A is the carotene pigment found in animal feeds (grass, silage, grass meal, carrots).

★ **Vitamin D, or Calciferol.** Contained in fish oil, baker's yeast, and hay flour.

★ **Vitamin E, or Tocopherol.** Contained in herbal flour, egg yolk, and milk. This vitamin is the key to longevity. Vitamin E affects the fertility, incubation quality, and nervous activity of poultry.

★ **Vitamin K.** Increases blood coagulation. Green fodder is rich in Vitamin K, and it is also found in root crops, like carrots and turnips. The absence or deficiency of vitamin K in the diet of poultry leads to serious diseases.

★ **B-group vitamins.** The effects of each type of vitamin B on the body are similar, but each vitamin is unique:

☆ **Vitamin B1.** Participates in carbohydrate metabolism and regulates the functions of the nervous system and cardiac activity.

☆ **Vitamin B2.** Responsible for tissue respiration intensity. It is involved in carbohydrate and fat metabolism. Essential for hemoglobin synthesis.

☆ **Vitamin B3.** Contained in wheat bran, yeast, grass meal, and legumes. It plays an important role in fat metabolism and affects the endocrine and nervous systems.

☆ **Vitamin B4.** Contained in yeast and cereal grains.

☆ **Vitamin B5, or nicotinic acid.** Participates in protein and carbohydrate metabolism.

☆ **Vitamin B6.** Participates in hemoglobin synthesis and protein metabolism.

☆ **Vitamin B12, or cyanocobalamin.** Participates in hematopoiesis and fat and carbohydrate metabolism. Contained exclusively in animal feed.

★ **Folic acid.** This plays a role in blood cell formation. It's contained in yeast and the green leaves of plants.

★ **Vitamin H, or Biotin.** This has a major influence on the skin. It's isolated from chicken egg yolks. Vitamin H is found in yeast, dairy products, molasses, and herbs. With its absence or deficiency in hens, the incubation of eggs decreases and skin diseases (dermatitis) appear.

SIGNS OF VITAMIN DEFICIENCY

★ **Vitamin A deficiency.** Metabolism reduction, egg production decreasing, poor growth. With this vitamin deficiency, egg yolks are a light yellow color, and hens have a dry cornea.

★ **Vitamin D deficiency.** Egg production reduction, poor poultry growth, bone deformation, rickets. To determine whether or not chickens have vitamin D deficiency is very simple: if the eggshell is very thin, soft, or even completely absent, a deficiency is likely.

★ **Vitamin E deficiency.** Shyness, higher anxiety, frequent appearance of unfertilized eggs in laying hens. Roosters become sterile. Chicks don't hatch when eggs are put in an incubator.

★ **Vitamin C.** Participates in all parts of the metabolism, the synthesis of hormones, and the neutralization of toxic substances. The hen's body synthesizes this vitamin. Needles and green fodder are rich in vitamin C.

DID YOU KNOW? The history of vitamin discovery is most directly related to poultry farming.

In 1895, Aikman, a doctor at a prison hospital located on the island of Java, discovered that chickens bred in prisons were also affected by the beriberi disease that afflicted the poor in China, Japan, and Indonesia. The diet of these chickens included only milled rice. When he added bran into their feed, the birds recovered. So thanks to hens, vitamin B1 was discovered, which highly affects carbohydrate metabolism.

★ **Vitamins B deficiency.** Causes muscle tissue damage, the underdevelopment of feathers and claws, poor growth, skin diseases, heart problems, and heart attacks.

★ **Vitamin K deficiency.** Leads to intramuscular bleeding and poor blood coagulation.

Vitamin feed is an essential part of the hen's diet. The main source of vitamins for poultry is greens. Greens are given to them only fresh, immediately after mowing in a crushed form.

Usually, 5–10 grams of greens should be given to every chick every day, and 20–30 grams per day to every adult hen.

Feeding hens with fresh herbs isn't easy, so most often, poultry is given green food in the form of hay or grass meal, which preserves almost all the nutritious properties of the fresh herbs.

As a green food, hens can be given all legumes and cereal plants, as well as a meadow, steppe, and forest herbs.

Green fodder should be mowed only in ecologically clean areas, in the forest, or in personal plots. It is undesirable to collect plants in industrial facilities areas, as well as near the roads with heavy traffic. You have to be careful when you're feeding poultry greens, making sure those greens haven't been treated with chemicals used to kill weeds.

In fall and winter, flocks are fed grass and coniferous flour, which get added to the main feed mixture.

CAUTION! It should be noted that such wild herbs as wormwood, tarragon, and dandelion should be fed to hens with caution. If these plants are given to poultry in large quantities, they can have a negative effect on some functions of their bodies.

VITAMINS PER 1 KG OF FEED

	A	D	E	K₃	B₁	B₂	B₆	B₁₂	Biotin	Folic acid	Nicotinic acid	Panto-thenic acid	Choline
	IU	IU	mg	mg	mg	mg	mg	mcg	mcg	mg	mg	mg	mg
Chicks 1–10 days	12k–16k	2.5k–3k	35–40	2–3	1–3	6–10	4–6	20–40	80–120	0.5–1.5	30–60	8–15	500–700
Chicks 2–5 weeks	8k–10k	1.5k–2k	15–20	1–2	2–3	3–6	2–5	10–20	40–60	0.5–1	30–60	6–10	300–500
Laying hens	8k–12k	2k–2.5k	15–25	1–2	2–3	5–8	3–5	15–25	40–60	0.5–1	30–50	6–12	400
Broilers	8k–12k	2k–4k	30–60	1–2	2–3	4–8	3–5	15–25	80–120	0.5–1	30–60	6–12	400–600
Turkeys	8k–12k	2k–3k	20–40	1–2	2–3	4–6	3–5	15–30	100–200	0.5–1	40–60	10–15	1k–1.5k

For Vitamin A: 1 IU* is the biological equivalent of 0.3 mcg retinol, or of 0.6 mcg beta-carotene.
For Vitamin D: 1 IU is the biological equivalent of 0.025 mcg cholecalciferol or ergocalciferol.

CAUTION! Laying hens that are kept in cages and don't have the space to walk around should receive feed with a high vitamin concentration.

*IU (international unit): An international unit (IU) is an internationally accepted amount of a substance. This type of measure is used for the fat-soluble vitamins (such as vitamins A, D and E) and certain hormones, enzymes, and biologicals (such as vaccines).

MINERAL SUPPLEMENTS

For normal metabolism, hens need minerals. The content of potassium, calcium, magnesium, sodium, chlorine, phosphorus, iron, manganese, fluorine, and iodine compounds in the feed determines its value.

Minerals such as sodium, phosphorus, and calcium are especially important for the life of the poultry. Calcium is necessary for skeleton and eggshell formation. It is perfectly absorbed with phosphorus in a 2:1 ratio. With a lack of calcium, eggs have no eggshell, and the bird can get sick.

★ **Chalk.** This is a white powder with lumps of various shapes. It contains calcium — 37%, phosphorus — 0.18%, potassium — 0.5%, sodium — 0.3%, silicon and other elements (no more than 5%).

CAUTION! Limestone with a peat mixture should not be used for poultry!

★ **Limestone.** This contains 33% calcium, 2% magnesium, 4% silicon, and a small amount of phosphorus, iron, sulfur, etc.

★ **Phosphorus** (P). This is part of the bone tissue along with calcium. Phosphorus is found in meat-bone and bone meal, fishmeal, yeast and other food of animal-origin.

★ **Calcium** (Ca). This is the most important component of the bone tissue of the hen's skeleton. Also, calcium is part of the nerve cells of muscle tissue and blood. Poultry kept on a grain feed periodically have a lack of calcium. Therefore, mineral supplements (eggshell, chalk, meat-bone meal and bone meal), as well as fodder yeast and dairy products should be included in the poultry diet.

★ **Magnesium** (Mg). This is a part of the skeleton bone tissue of poultry along with calcium and phosphorus but in a smaller amount. With a balanced diet, hens usually have enough magnesium.

★ **Potassium** (K). Participates in protein metabolism, is part of the cell fluid, and regulates the water percent in tissues. Potassium is found in fodder yeast, wheat bran, and legume pods.

★ **Sodium (Na) and chlorine (Cl)— Salt.** Helps maintain the osmotic pressure in the cells and tissues of the body, which are part of the blood. Sodium and chlorine are most often given to poultry as sodium chloride **(NaCl),** one to two times a week, in very small doses.

★ **Copper (Cu).** Participates in redox processes of tissues and in the hemoglobin formation in the blood. If the diet of hens does not have enough feed containing this element, it must be added every two months with drinking water (add two to three crystals of copper sulfate to the water).

★ **Iron (Fe).** Participates in the hemoglobin synthesis and in redox metabolic processes. High iron levels are found in meat-bone, fish meal, and wheat bran. Iron is also present in many types of grain feed.

★ **Sulfur (S).** This is part of many organic compounds necessary for normal body functioning. Skimmed milk powder, peas, and meat-bone meal are rich in these amino acids. In addition, cysteine and methionine are found in cereal feed.

★ **Iodine (I).** This is part of the thyroxine hormone, which is produced by the thyroid gland. Iodine is found in many feeds; therefore, with a varied diet, poultry should get enough of it.

★ **Molybdenum (Mo) and selenium (Se).** They are part of some enzymes. These elements are found in all types of grain feed.

★ **Shells.** Shells are washed and freed from shellfish meat, which can also be used as food, and shells are crushed and ground. There is a lot of calcium in shells, and 0.5 kg of shells will replace 1 kg of chalk.

★ **Eggshell.** This is an affordable and good mineral nutrition. Before feeding it must be boiled, dried, and crushed.

★ **Gravel.** The flock should constantly have gravel in the feeders or on the paddock — finely divided minerals or stones of various compositions. The hens prefer quartz or granite stones.

> **CAUTION! In the absence of gravel, chickens can swallow coal, pieces of brick, glass, and other objects, which can be dangerous to their health.**

In the poultry's stomach, gravel promotes feed grinding and digestion. The absence or deficiency of it leads to incomplete absorption of the nutrients contained in the feed.

In a ratio, these substances are put at the rate of 5% of the total mass of feed. Most often, farmers only use chalk as a supplement.

Properly selected feed supplements will allow hens to feel good, and they will delight you with high-quality, strong eggs.

LIFE HACK ALERT! It is recommended to give a hen 50% of a calcium supplement after 14–15 hours of the day — this is a practice that best suits the timing of the natural process of egg formation. In this case, the shell will be better and stronger.

CAUTION! Keep in mind that in pure form, chalk cannot be given to hens. It is important to mix it with food. The reason for this is the poor salivary glands development of hens, which is why hens cannot normally swallow this substance. At the same time, chalk should not be the only source of calcium because it will cause hens to eat less food.

COMPOUND FEED

Compound feed is a feed mixture prepared according to the species, age, breed, and productive differences of the bird. A combined feed is produced industrially. Compound feed is actively used for feeding hens and other types of poultry. Rationally formulated ready-made feed mixtures reduce feed costs.

While it is certainly possible to feed poultry a diet consisting entirely of wheat or mixed corn, this will not provide birds with all the essential nutrients in the correct balance to suit the birds' particular stages of life. The advantage of feeding a complete or compound feed is that all the work of calculating the best combination of quality ingredients to provide a natural, healthy diet that fulfils the bird's nutritional requirements has been done for you. For the poultry keeper, this means that you can feed your birds confidently, with the knowledge that you will be providing them with everything necessary for a healthy and productive life, but in a form that's convenient and easy to use. These feeds are readily available to suit chicks, growing birds, breeding birds, and layers, and depending on the purpose may be available as crumbs, pellets, or meal.

For sure it's almost impossible to use all of the above types of feed, so I just described as many feed types as possible so that you can choose what is most convenient for you. I have at one point tried each of them, but I don't use them all now. I've constructed a feeding program that I consider the most effective. It is important to draw up a diet in such a way that your chickens' nutrition is balanced and includes as many elements as necessary for their full development. Below I give an example of the feeding program that I use in my household.

FEEDING PROGRAMS FOR LAYING HENS, CHICKENS AND BROILERS

If you properly organize the diet for your flock, they will be able to lay eggs year-round. It is best to use a combined method of feeding, including flour mixture, whole grains, vegetable and animal feed, as well as mineral supplements.

APPROXIMATE SEASONAL DIET FOR HENS (GRAMS PER HEN/DAY):				
Feed	Autumn	Winter	Spring	Summer
Grain	60	70	75	75
Wheat bran	25	25	25	25
Fish and meat-bone meal	2	3	7	5
Carrot	-	30	-	-
Green feed	40	-	40	40
Root vegetables and boiled potatoes	100	100	100	-
Chalk, eggshell	3	5	6	6
Salt	1	1	1	1

ESTIMATED HEN'S ENERGY AND NUTRIENTS REQUIREMENTS (PER HEN/DAY):

Exchange energy, kcal	Protein, g	Calcium, g	Phosphorus, g	Sodium, g
FOR BROILERS				
341	25,6	4,48	1,2	0,48
418	24,8	4,34	1,09	0,47
385	21,0	4,05	1,05	0,45
377	20,3	3,91	1,01	0,43
FOR MEAT-EGG HENS:				
305	19,2	3,50	0,79	0,34
304	18,72	3,63	0,82	0,35
FOR LAYING HENS:				
324	20,4	3,72	0,84	0,36

AN APPROXIMATE DAILY DIET FOR LAYING HENS:

Feed	Grams per hen/day
Grain (oats, wheat, barley, etc.)	50
Flour mixture	50
Hay flour	10
Succulent feed	30–50
Dry protein feed of plant and animal origin	10–15
Shell	5
Bone meal	2
Salt	0,5

AN APPROXIMATE DAILY DIET FOR MEAT-EGG HENS:

Feed	Grams per hen/day
Whole grain (3–5 types)	50
Grain-Flour mixture (3–5 types)	50
Wheat bran	10
Sunflower seeds	5
Meat-Bone and fish meal	10–15
Herbal flour (hay, coniferous)	5
Carrot, cabbage leaves, pumpkin	40
Crushed shell or chalk	5
Salt	0,7

AN APPROXIMATE DAILY DIET FOR BROILERS:

Feed	% of the total diet
Ground grain	75–80
Plant-based protein feed	12–16
Protein feed of animal origin	5–6
Herbal flour	1–2
Animal fat	3
Crushed shell or chalk	2
Salt	0,5–1

AN APPROXIMATE DAILY DIET FOR CHICKS: (GRAMS PER CHICK/DAY)

Age (days)	Boiled egg	Milk	Skim cheese	Cereal	Sunflower seeds	Greens or carrots	Boiled potatoes	Meat-bone or fish meal	Mineral feed	Salt
1–5	2	5	1	5	0	1	0	0	0	0
6–10	3	10	2	12	1	5	0	1	0,5	0
11–20	0	20	3	25	2	10	5	2	1	0
21–30	0	25	4	40	2	12	15	3	2	0
31–40	0	30	5	50	3	15	20	4	2	0,1
41–50	0	35	5	65	3	20	30	5	3	0,2
51–60	0	35	6	80	4	25	40	7	3	0,3

DRINKING WATER

Water is essential for all living organisms and contributes to all life processes, helping with the absorption of nutrients. Filtered water is the best solution for poultry.

Poultry water needs depend on many factors — ambient temperature, body temperature, food intake, etc.

A bird's water consumption increases during its growth. In addition, water consumption increases if birds are fed only with grain feed, and slightly decreases if juicier feed is present in their diet.

In some diseases, for example, with an intestinal upset, birds need to be given as much drinking water as possible, since frequent secretions lead the body to a forced loss of fluid that can cause dehydration.

After washing the coop and before the chickens' arrival, it is necessary to check the water for the presence of bacterial infection. The sheet below shows the maximum permissible content of minerals and organic substances in water.

LIFE HACK ALERT! The decisive factor for good poultry health is aquatic hygiene. The water in the drinkers must be changed every day, while the drinkers must be washed thoroughly.

CAUTION! If adding liquid or powdered vitamins to water, water must be changed every 10–12 hours, since all vitamin supplements contain substances that promote the rapid multiplication of bacteria.

RECAP

★ Feed consists of **organic substances, minerals,** and **water.** Organic substances include protein, carbohydrates, fats, and vitamins. It's extremely important that chickens have a balanced diet.

★ **Protein feeds:** dairy products, fish or fishmeal, meat and bone meal, chicken egg, earthworms, fly larvae, crank, June bugs, soy, peas, wheat bran.

★ **Carbohydrate feeds:** corn, oats, wheat, rye, barley, millet, potato, carrot, turnip, pumpkin, cabbage.

★ **Fats:** by origin, they are divided into animal and plant fats and contained in various foods.

★ **Vitamin feed:** Vitamin A or retinol, Vitamin D or Calciferol, Vitamin E or Tocopherol, Vitamin K, B-group vitamins, Folic acid, Vitamin H or Biotin, Vitamin C.

★ **Mineral supplements:** Chalk, Limestone, Phosphorus (P), Calcium (Ca), Magnesium (Mg), Potassium (K), Sodium (Na) and chlorine (Cl) — Salt, Copper (Cu), Iron (Fe), Sulfur (S), Iodine (I), Molybdenum (Mo), Selenium (Se), Shells, Eggshell, Gravel.

★ **Compound feed.** Rationally formulated, ready-made feed mixtures reduce the cost of feed and make the feed preparation process easier.

★ Check the water for bacterial and mineral pollution regularly.

★ Ensure unrestricted access to fresh, clean, and high-quality feed and water.

NOTES

65

BREEDING AND RAISING CHICKENS

BREEDING CHICKENS IS cost-effective work that will yield healthy eggs and meat for your whole family. In a private household, it is better to constantly keep young livestock, which can either be acquired or hatched independently.

EGG INCUBATION

Chicks are made in two ways: under a brood hen and through incubators. Egg laying for incubation is carried out in March and April. If natural incubation is used, then the eggs are laid under the hen. In this case, the hen is first set down on eggs, because, among modern breeds of hens, not everyone has an incubation instinct.

There are several rules:

★ First, the hen should cover all laid eggs with his body;

★ Second, the number of the laid eggs should be odd, as in this case they are better distributed under the brood hen.

LIFE HACK ALERT!
Chicken eggs don't have to be laid under a brood of this particular species. For example, turkeys are excellent brood hens. Even males can hatch eggs. Goose, duck, and chicken eggs, as well as pheasant eggs, can be placed under a turkey.

CAUTION! It is unacceptable to leave eggs for a long time in the nest because this can provoke the hatching instinct in the female and thereby reduce the egg production. Also, poultry may develop an egg-pecking habit.

A laid egg has almost the same temperature as the hen's body. During cooling, an air chamber appears on the dull end of the egg, where air penetrates through the shell pores. Together with air, microbes and mold spores can get into the egg, which will cause the death of the embryo. Therefore, eggs collected while they're still warm should be allowed to cool in a cool, dry room.

Moreover, keeping eggs in the nest for too long in the summer reduces the incubation quality, and in the winter, it leads to eggs overcooling.

When an egg is heavily soiled and it is intended for incubation, it should be washed. Do this very carefully. Use a 1% hydrogen peroxide solution or a weak potassium permanganate solution. Before this cleaning, put the eggs in clean water with a temperature of 9°F higher than that of the eggs.

For incubation, select eggs laid before 8 am. They must be of regular oval shape and cannot have shell defects. Defective chicks are most often hatched from eggs of irregular (round, too elongated, squeezed) shape, and cracked shells disrupt gas and water exchange.

Under the eggshell is a protein, and inside it is a yolk, which contains all the substances necessary for embryo development. The shell has many microscopic pores. Gas exchange is carried out through them. A fresh egg has a dull surface since the shell is covered with a very thin supershell membrane, which protects the egg against pathogenic microbes from penetrating it.

To select eggs for breeding, check them under a light. Eggs suitable for incubation have a uniformly translucent shell and a dark yolk, which is located in the center. When you rotate the egg, the yolk should slowly move.

Collect more eggs for several days of further incubation. Store collected eggs in a cool (not higher than 54°F), dry (relative humidity not higher than 75–80%) room in a horizontal position and periodically turn them over.

After a week of nesting, the eggs should be re-scanned in the light. The fullness of the egg is determined by the presence of the embryo: a dark speck with branches extending in different directions, gradually thinning. If an egg is clear when viewed under a light, it is unfertilized, and if a blood ring or gyrus is visible, then the embryo development has stopped.

If you have a mercury-vapor lamp, egg irradiation can be used. This method increases the embryo viability and stimulates its development chances since under the rays vitamin D is formed. For irradiation, the lamp is installed at a distance of at least 15". This procedure should last from two to thirty minutes.

Having chosen a brood hen, clear some feathers from a part of her abdomen and use them to line the bottom of the nest. When the eggs come into contact with the hen, this enhances heat transfer. From time to time, when the hen becomes hot, it rises from the nest and turns the eggs with the cold side up.

For incubation, choose a clean, darkened room without extraneous odors.

CAUTION! With long-term egg storage, the number of potential broods decreases. Therefore, the earlier the egg is laid under the brood hen or in the incubator, the more chances you'll get chickens.

An Example of a Healthy Egg Under a Light

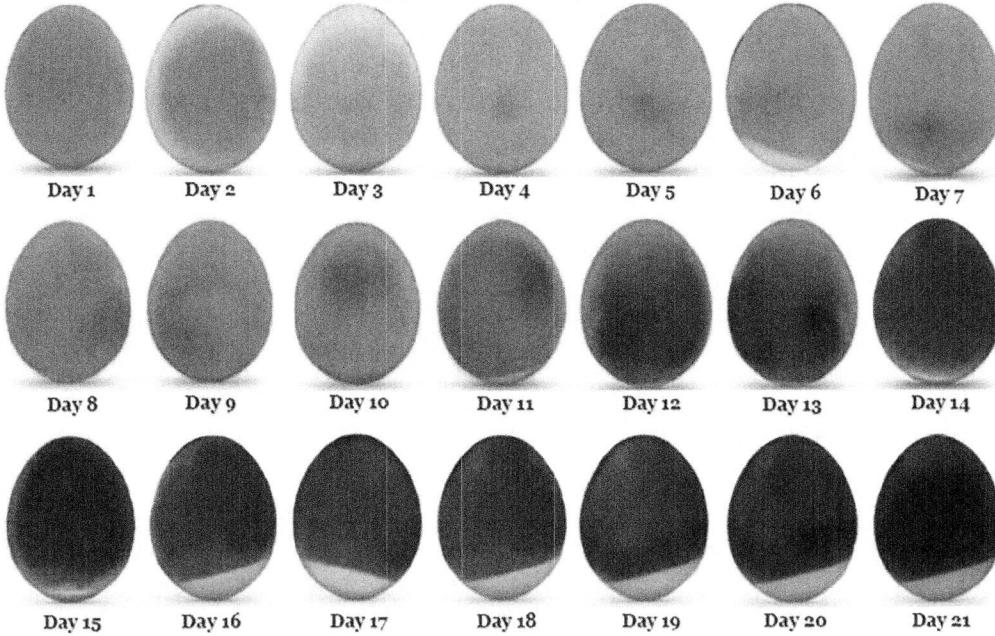

Day 1	Day 2	Day 3	Day 4	Day 5	Day 6	Day 7
Day 8	Day 9	Day 10	Day 11	Day 12	Day 13	Day 14
Day 15	Day 16	Day 17	Day 18	Day 19	Day 20	Day 21

The temperature of the room should be at least 54°F. In addition, the room should be quiet. For this, the hens are kept separate from the rest of the birds.

The coop, where the hens are placed, must be cleaned and aired daily. If the weather is cold, the room should be warmed up from time to time. Nests need to be inspected regularly to remove broken eggs in time, you need to regularly change the litter. In this case, you need to try not to bother the hens too much.

Chick hatching begins one day before the hatch itself. The hens will become restless, and you'll hear the sound of beaks tapping on the shell (you can hear

LIFE HACK ALERT! If necessary, to extend the storage time life and to increase the embryo vitality, use the following method. Place the eggs in an incubator for five hours (air temperature 100°F, relative humidity 70%). After five hours, place the warm eggs in a cool room and store them for up to fifteen days. This procedure should be performed no earlier than the second and no later than the fourth day after the egg collection.

it if you bring the egg to your ear). Rising, the bird passes the hatched chick to the edge of the nest. Chickens are usually hatched on the 21st day of incubation.

For the successful use of home incubators, it is necessary to know the incubation microclimate, which depends not only on the species but also on the poultry breed.

One of the main parameters of incubation is temperature. Sudden temperature changes are detrimental to the embryo; therefore, you need to constantly monitor the temperature and prevent eggs from overheating or overcooling. The thermometer in the incubator should be positioned so that is just above the eggs. The incoming air passes through the ventilation hole below, so the temperature under the eggs is slightly lower.

The second parameter of incubation is humidity. It is directly dependent on the water evaporation through the shell, which affects the metabolism inside the egg. The incubator must be well ventilated to ensure normal oxygen supply and a timely removal of gas exchange products.

The eggs selected for placement in the incubator should be placed in a tray. By this time, all necessary conditions must be passed.

From the first to the fifteenth day, the eggs require more heat and increased humidity. Then, before the hatching begins, temperature and humidity are reduced, and ventilation is increased. During the hatching, humidity and ventilation are also increased. The hatching period begins when the chicks in the eggs begin to make sounds.

DID YOU KNOW? Artificial incubation has been used for a long time. In Ancient Egypt, more than three thousand years ago, for example, it was a monopoly of the priests of Osiris. According to archaeologists, the ancient incubator was a long, two-story building, divided into cubicles and without windows. The eggs were laid on the first floor and were heated by straw burned on the second floor. Artificial incubation was also used in Ancient China: eggs were placed in special ovens — kangs — or in trenches, then covered with heated rice husk.

In Europe, artificial incubation began to be used only in the XVIII century. The first models of incubators were designed by the French physicist Reaumur. At the beginning of the XX century. incubators were spread to industrial poultry, and in the second half of the last century, in domestic.

The eggs in the trays need to be regularly turned over. Otherwise, the embryo may die. When using homemade incubators that are not equipped with devices for turning eggs, this operation is combined with a cooling procedure and carried out two to three times a day by hand. Egg cooling begins on the second day of incubation and ends immediately before hatching begins.

In the egg, the chicken is in a bent position, and the head lies under the right-wing. Before leaving the egg, the chick pecks the shell and begins to squeak.

After hatching, a healthy chick should look clean. He must be able to stand firm on his feet, walk well, be active, and be mobile. It should have a fully absorbed yolk and a healed navel, as well as no deformities.

For breeding, one rooster is left for eleven to twelve chickens.

LIFE HACK ALERT! You can check the adequacy of cooling by holding the egg to your eyelid. Cooling is normal if you feel neither heat nor cold.

LIFE HACK ALERT! The chick should make a satisfied squeak.

FEEDING

The main goal of proper feeding is to stimulate the early feed and water intake. This will allow you to achieve a maximum weight faster with strong characteristics of well-being and egg laying.

After hatching, the chicks must be provided with optimal conditions that satisfy all physiological and food needs. This ensures the early development of feed and water consumption, the optimal development of the intestines and other organs, and the development of the skeleton to maintain muscle growth during the entire growth process.

At the last stage of incubation and immediately after hatching, the chicken receives all the necessary nutrients from the yolk. After arriving at the farm, the chicken begins to receive all the nutrients from

LIFE HACK ALERT! Watch the newly hatched chickens. You'll see them pecking and looking for food early on.

the feed in the form of sifted grains or mini-granules from the feeders, as well as a paper spread on the floor with a feed.

It is impossible to feed chicks on an empty floor. Otherwise, they will catch a cold.

For the first ten days, chicks are fed every two hours. During this period, the finest chopped, boiled eggs, crumbly cottage cheese mixed with semolina or corn grits will be the best food for them. For ten chicks, give one egg or 50 g of cottage cheese mixed with 50 g of cereal. It is useful to give chicks small amounts of cereal, slightly crushed flakes, adding milk powder (1/4 part of the volume of cereals) and one crushed tablet of multivitamins (per ten chicks).

After each feeding, check whether all chicks have a full goiter. If there are chickens with an incomplete goiter, they must be transferred to another room and fed separately.

Checking for goiter fullness:

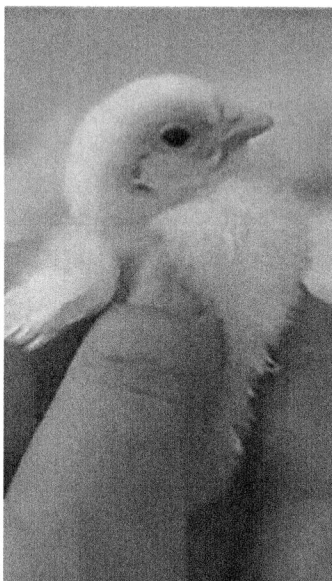

LIFE HACK ALERT! For the first three to five days, it is better for chicks to lay paper on the floor, and put sifted chicken feed, small corn grits on it. Chicks are dug in such a litter without harming themselves and stay clean.

CAUTION! In no case should chickens get into their feeders and drinkers: contaminated food and water cause intestinal diseases, and wet litter is fatal for immature chickens.

LIFE HACK ALERT! Such a dry mixture is convenient in that the poultry breeder can go away for a long time, filling the feed in the feeder, and the chickens themselves regulate the feed intake.

From three to five days of age, chicks should be taught to eat finely chopped, fresh herbs, like alfalfa, clover, nettle, etc. And at five to seven days of age, it is good to give loose mixes of yogurt, meat and fish broth, as well as meat and fish waste (5–7 g each). On the tenth day, give them boiled potatoes, grated carrots, pumpkin, zucchini, and other vegetables. Wet loose mixtures should be eaten for 30–40 minutes (30–40 g per each chick).

Fresh sour-milk products are very useful for the chicks' intestines. As a disinfectant, two times a week for half an hour, give them a weak solution of potassium permanganate, but you should not give it immediately without a need for it in the first days of their life.

From ten days of age, chicks can be given finely crushed chalk and well-boiled, ground eggshells. In separate feeders, there should always be fine gravel or coarse sand. It is also necessary to provide the chicks with continuous access to fresh clean water at the recommended height (see "Drinkers" chapter). Water needs to be changed several times a day.

The feeders and drinkers number should be sufficient; otherwise, chicks will interfere with each other.

CAUTION! This feed residues must be removed. (Acidified food causes poisoning and death of chickens).

MICROCLIMATE

In the first month, especially the first ten days, chickens need special care. They need a warm, dry, clean room with good ventilation, but without drafts. On ten square feet you should place no more than 20–25 chickens. After 4.5 weeks, they are seated for seventeen chicks, and, starting from ten to twenty weeks, ten chicks per one square foot. Care must be taken to ensure that the air in this place is ventilated, but strong drafts are undesirable.

At the initial stage, as a chick house, you can use a cardboard box, a wooden box, or a special cage.

The chicks should be located somewhere that:

⭐ Is dry and clean;

⭐ Has proper temperature and humidity;

⭐ Has proper lighting and ventilation.

The microclimate for young chickens age (temperature, relative humidity, litter, water, and food) should allow the chicken to adapt to new conditions in order to start actively consuming food and water as soon as possible. For the first time after hatching, the residual yolk is a kind of reserve of nutrients until the food will be given. If the chicken begins to receive food immediately after hatching, it will begin to develop immediately and the residual yolk will be activated when the feed enters the intestines, thereby providing an additional incentive for development. If the chicken does not start receiving food immediately after hatching, it receives nutrients only from the residual yolk, which slows its development. A herd where chickens did not begin to consume food within one, two, or three days after hatching develops more slowly.

Young chickens are not able to regulate their body temperature until they reach the age of about twelve to fourteen days. Favorable body temperature must be ensured by creating optimal air temperature. The temperature of the floor is extremely important for young chickens, as is the temperature of the air, so you should preheat the chick houses.

In the first five days, the temperature in the chick house should be 84–86°F. On the sixth day, it can be reduced to 78–82°F, and after that, decrease by 5°F every week. by the end of the month it can be brought to 64°F. It is good to heat chicks with infrared lamps: they do not blind and can be left overnight. In warm, sunny weather, chickens can be taken outside from when they're three days old, but it should be done gradually.

Recommended microclimate for chickens:

★ **Air temperature** 86°F (should be measured at the chicken's height or at the point of placement of feed and water);

★ **Floor temperature** 82–86°F;

★ **Relative humidity** 60–70%.

LIFE HACK ALERT! Litter thickness of less than four inches is not recommended, as it does not create the necessary insulation of the cold floor of the house and has lower moisture absorption, which leads to increased contact of chickens with droppings. Insufficient litter thickness also leads to increased condensation from the floor. In geographic regions that have a cold winter, it is recommended to use a litter four inches thick, even with a longer coop heating period.

Before the chickens hatch, spread the litter material with an even layer that's two to four inches thick. Rough bedding may limit chicks' access to feed and water. At the optimum floor temperature (82–86°F), a minimum litter thickness of two inches can be used.

Lighting is also a very important factor for chickens. Newborn chicks require around-the-clock light. After two weeks, the directions change: sixteen to seventeen hours of light are needed for the meat breeds and eight hours for the egg breeds.

OBSERVING CHICKEN BEHAVIOR

The most effective indicator of the optimal conditions for keeping chickens is regular and careful monitoring of their behavior. The general rule is that if the chickens are evenly distributed throughout the coop area, this means that they feel comfortable and there is no need to adjust the microclimate conditions.

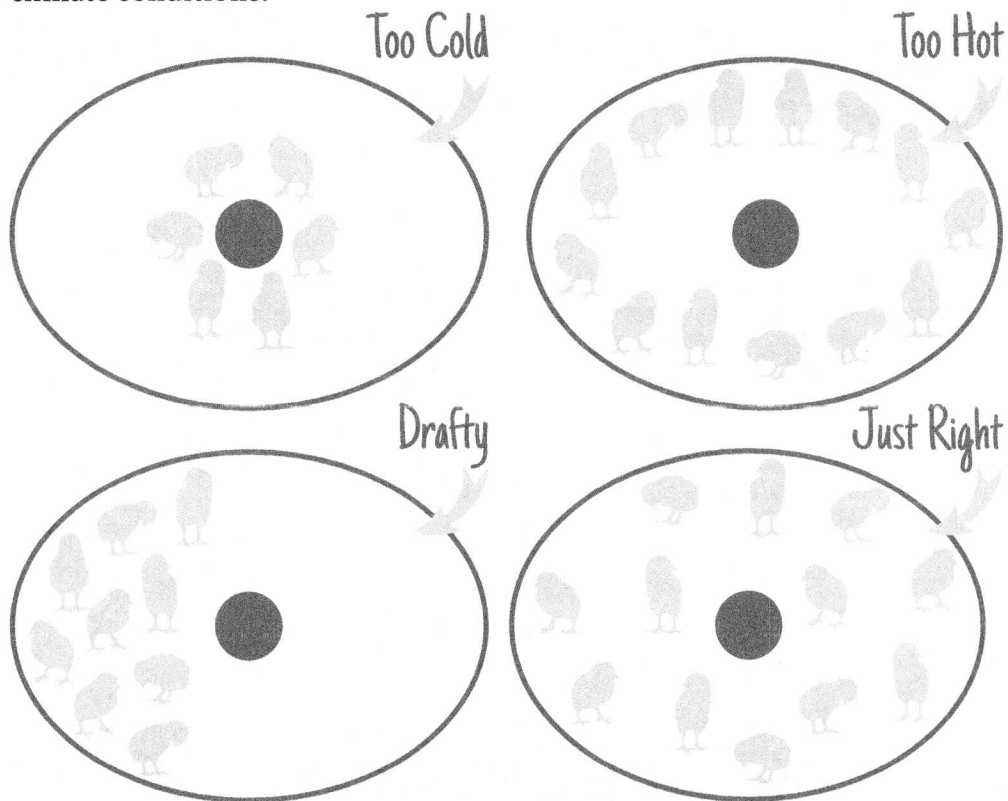

Too Cold

Too Hot

Drafty

Just Right

Therefore, you should regularly and carefully monitor the behavior of chickens. When behavior changes, adjust the temperature and humidity accordingly.

RECAP

★ Chicks are made in two ways: under a broody hen and through incubators.

★ For the incubation, eggs must be of regular oval shape and not have shell defects. To select eggs, checking them under a light. Eggs suitable for incubation have a uniformly translucent shell and a dark yolk, located in the center.

★ After a week of nesting, re-check the eggs under the light. The fullness of the egg is determined by the presence of the embryo.

★ Chickens are usually hatched on the twenty-first day of incubation.

★ For breeding, one rooster is left for eleven to twelve chickens.

★ The main goal of proper feeding is to stimulate early feed and water intake.

★ It is impossible to feed chicks on an empty floor. Otherwise, they will catch a cold.

★ The main requirements for where you keep your chicks:

☆ Dry and clean;

☆ Proper temperature and humidity;

☆ Correct lighting and ventilation mode.

★ Recommended microclimate for chickens:

☆ Air temperature 86°F (should be measured at the chicken's height or at the point of placement of feed and water);

☆ Floor temperature 82–86°F;

☆ Relative humidity 60–70%.

NOTES

HOW TO PREPARE HENS FOR THE WINTER

BEFORE PLACING THE poultry in the winter premises, the chicken coop needs to be sanitized. To do this, it is recommended to treat the walls and floor with lime (at the rate of 2 kg. of lime per 10-liter bucket of water). Some farmers use a blowtorch to disinfect.

STEP 1 — COOP INSULATION

The winter coop should not have gaps where cold air can penetrate. Therefore, carefully close them, close any holes tightly, and on the floor, build a thick enough litter of straw, dry sawdust, coconut fiber, or peat. When the first layer is trampled, lay a new one. So you need to make several layers. This will be enough to ensure that in winter the air temperature in the chicken coop reaches 53°F to 64°F. At this temperature, hens feel quite comfortable and will continue to lay eggs.

If the winter turns out to be very frosty, then install additional heaters. In this case, it is necessary to ensure the fresh air is coming to the henhouse, and the perches where the chickens sleep should be at least 23" above the floor.

STEP 2 — LIGHTING

The greatest egg production in laying hens falls on the period when daylight hours are equal to fourteen to eighteen hours. To achieve this result when keeping chickens in winter, you need to artificially increase daylight hours by installing additional lighting in the chicken coop.

Typically, lighting is turned on from 6:00 a.m. until 9:00 a.m., and from about 5:00 p.m. until 8:00 p.m.–8:30 p.m.

These measures are optimal, but you also can choose not to use additional lighting. In this case, the hen's productivity will be less.

LIFE HACK ALERT! The temperature in the coop should not exceed 64°F, and humidity, 70%. At low air temperature — 40°F, productivity decreases by 15%, at too high — up to 86°F — by 30%.

CAUTION! It is only necessary to use fluorescent lamps, as ordinary incandescent lamps will not create the desired effect. It is necessary to arrange the lamps so that the chickens cannot damage them.

LIFE HACK ALERT! Laying hens are very susceptible to stress, so if there is a power outage in your area, you need to install a backup power station that will provide uninterrupted electricity supply.

STEP 3 – FEEDING

Both the physical state of the hens and their egg production depend on nutrition. In fall and winter, chickens require more thorough care, so even before the onset of cold weather take care not only to prepare the henhouse but also the feed.

Harvest dried grass, or clover, in summer. It is also worth to pre-harvest branch feed (branches). It is best to use branches of yellow acacia, birch, or linden. Cut branches up to thirty inches in length are tied together in eight to ten pieces and hung under a canopy, in the shade side. In five days, these brooms can be put (it is better to hang) in storage.

For one hen left for the winter, it is necessary to prepare up to eight kilograms of hay and up to twenty brooms. It will be an excellent vitamin feed supplement.

In addition to cereals, poultry diets should also include root crops: pumpkin, carrots, beets, zucchini, or potatoes. It is better to give it in a boiled form. The lack of greenery is compensated by adding vitamin D.

It's very good if you can add worms to the hen's diet. They provide hens with protein and calcium.

In separate containers in the coop, there should be crushed mollusk shells, chalk, fine gravel, and pebbles. Be sure to have drinking water. In winter, water needs to be slightly warmed up. Keep your drinkers clean.

LIFE HACK ALERT! The largest percentage of laying hens diet is the cereals: wheat, barley, or corn. Before feeding, the grain must be crushed. You can also give germinated grains.

CAUTION! If the eggshell is soft, this means a lack of calcium. In this case, increase the content of this mineral in the poultry diet.

LIFE HACK ALERT! The useful feeding, the so-called mishmash. Cooking is easy. Just add bran, eggshell, bone or fish meal, sunflower meal, and mixed them all. Mishmash should not be given to hens in the evening. Give it to the hens in the morning and at lunchtime.

RECAP

★ **3 steps of successful hens keeping in winter:**

☆ **Coop insulation.** This will be enough to ensure that in winter the air temperature in the chicken coop reaches 53°F — 64°F;

☆ **Lighting.** Typically, lighting is turned on from 6:00 a.m. until 9:00 a.m., and from about 5:00 p.m. until 8:00 p.m. — 8:30 p.m.;

☆ **Feeding.** Both the physical state of the hens and their egg production depend on nutrition. In fall and winter, chickens require more thorough care.

NOTES

....
....
....
....
....
....
....
....
....
....
....
....
....

NOTES

HOW TO BUILD A COOP

BUILDING A BASIC chicken coop for a small flock of birds is a solid weekend project for the determined DIYer with basic carpentry skills. More elaborate coops could easily take several weeks (and will require advanced carpentry skills).

The internet is awash in guides for building backyard chicken coops. And the internet is a great place to look for inspiration. But let's keep it simple; all coops have two main components: an enclosed space for sleeping and laying eggs and an open air "chicken run," where chickens can roam around during the day. The enclosed space should open directly to the run, but should be elevated at least two feet above it, so there is space to collect the droppings that fall through the floor. (More on that in a moment.)

WHERE TO PLACE A COOP

When you're choosing a location for the future chicken coop, it's necessary to take into account sanitary, hygiene, and fire safety requirements, as well as where the coop is in relation to where you live. It should be about 30–50 feet from your living quarters.

The coop should be close to the person watching the hens because it'll save you time, facilitates the supervision of the bird, and help you protect the birds from all kinds of predators. There should be lawns for grazing and shrubs where poultry can hide from the sun and predators. Also, it's great to have a sandy place for "sand-swimming," where the sun freely penetrates, and large trees under which hens, digging and looking for worms, can occupy themselves for the whole day and remain in the shade and cool during the heat.

All of these conditions are desirable, but not required.

TYPES OF COOPS

There are many possible ways to configure a coop, I have found a few that work pretty well for a small flock.

If you're looking for something special, you can easily find many more detailed plans on the internet. Or just send me a query by email (you'll find my email at the end of the book), and I'll send you a few more detailed samples.

LIFE HACK ALERT! It is important to note that for the window, you will need double and preferably triple layers of glass.

CAUTION! Rodents (mice and rats) like to live near hens, so you can add a small metal mesh above the floor and walls to protect your coop.

If the total available area is very small, you can make the coop more compact by increasing the number of nests and perches. So to say, "add floors" one above the other. If you make a coop for laying hens, your hens will find this comfortable and cozy. Broilers have a tougher time with this, though, as they don't like to climb.

If winter weather requires coop warming, you can build a coop a half a meter above ground level with a window on the south side.

FOUNDATION

If you want to build a foundation for the coop, the most common types are made with poles or piles. But if the building is lightweight, you can use ready-made blocks, even in a homemade version. Particularly strong foundations are built only when the walls are made of heavy materials, such as bricks, foam blocks, cinder blocks, or a shell rock.

COLD PROTECTION

It is important to think in advance about coop insulation and heating. Since heating is a costly expense, it will be more profitable for you to take care of insulation in advance, so that in the future, there will be no additional heating costs.

Insulation of a chicken coop can be added both inside the walls and directly outside the walls. Inexpensive materials are fine to use.

Polyfoam* is used most often. It is lightweight, the cost is minimal, and the heat insulation is perfect. A two-inch-thick slab replaces a 20-inch brick wall. It's very easy to install. You can put the blocks on glue or nails with additional fixing washers, or just use improvised means.

Mineral wool, which is well suited for insulation, can also be used. But it requires additional costs for wind and moisture protection on the outside and steam protection on the inside of the walls.

* Polyfoam polyurethane (PUR) / polyisocyanurate (PIR) is one of the most effective insulation materials commonly available today. it is also extremely versatile and can be used just about anywhere.

LIFE HACK ALERT!
A very useful material is polystyrene foam. Because of its characteristics, it's better than polyfoam, and rodents avoid it. It also just looks good and doesn't require sheathing. As for cons? It comes at a fairly high cost.

87

You will also need to take care of the ceiling. If heat escapes from the ceiling of the coop, all of your efforts will be for naught. Cardboard keeps heat in well. You can place it on the surface, but it is better to use plywood* and leave sawdust or hay in the attic for better results.

Don't forget about the floor. It's better to seal the floors as much as possible. And by the way, a wooden floor isn't your only option. You can lay a mixture of clay with straw or concrete. Concrete floors are cold, so it's advised that you add an insulation layer to them.

Another way to avoid heating costs is to transform a vestibule or dresser into a simple coop. This significantly reduces the warm air loss when opening and closing doors.

* Plywood is a type of strong thin wooden board consisting of two or more layers glued and pressed together with the direction of the grain alternating.

LIFE HACK ALERT! The easiest way to regulate the humidity of the room: to increase it, you can install containers with water; to decrease, install an infrared lamp, which perfectly removes condensation.

CAUTION! For a coop illumination, it is advised to take thick glass and nets in order to protect the hens from being injured by pieces of glass when breaking the lamp.

VENTILATION

When you're constructing for coop ventilation, it is important to make sure there are no gaps in the coop, to prevent drafts. You'll probably want to mount a plastic under the ceiling with an exit through the roof.

It's possible to create an additional air vent at floor level. Your main objective is to protect all these holes from the rodents with a grid.

LIGHTING

The coop cannot do without a window on the south side. Yes, this lowers the temperature slightly, but the bird is a living organism that needs sunlight. In addition to at least double glass, it is important to provide the net with an aperture inside, for the flock's safety.

In winter, when daylight hours are shortened, add additional lighting to maintain good egg productivity.

LIFE HACK ALERT! Chickens do not perceive the violet part of the light spectrum, so the blue color for them is almost like darkness. Blue lamps are used in the coop to catch hens. And if the bird begins to behave somewhat aggressively and peck each other, then specialists recommend the brightness lowering of the lighting to solve this problem.

RECAP

★ Choose the right location to place a coop. It's necessary to take into account sanitary, hygiene, and fire safety requirements.

★ Choose the right construction of a coop and pay particular attention to:

☆ Foundation;

☆ Cold Protection;

☆ Ventilation;

☆ Lighting.

NOTES

HOW TO ADDRESS STRESS IN HENS

CHICKENS HAVE A highly organized nervous system. Watching them, you can see that chickens often quarrel and fight. Strong individuals repel weak ones from the feeders and don't always calmly sit on a perch. Humans have complex feelings and relationships, and birds are no different! The psychology of birds has not been studied enough, but a person can discover more about them by observing their behavior, the intonations of their voices, and the complex sounds that reflect the lives of chicken. Therefore, proper care of hens is the main measure to prevent stress.

LIFE HACK ALERT!
To check how birds feel in a coop, put a bed in there, and go to sleep there for one night. If you get up with a headache in the morning, don't spend money on feed and antibiotics until you adjust the ventilation and deal with all the other factors that provoke stress.

Stress can be caused by various irritants that occur mainly during fasting, a sharp diet change, cramped cage or indoors, poor microclimate, strong extraneous noise, a lack of drinkers or feeders, etc. It has been established that hens under stress see a decline in growth, development, and egg production. Stress can provoke many other disorders, which often lead to injury or death.

Consider some of the key factors that lead to flocks becoming depressed:

A HIGH POPULATION DENSITY IN THE COOP. This not only violates the microclimate and impedes access to water and feed but also deprives hens of peace and rest and injures their nervous system. Keep this in mind. A big mistake is keeping two roosters in the same coop, which leads to constant conflicts not only between roosters but also between hens.

Hens in a group can distinguish new members of their flock, and a new member usually leads to quarrels and attacks on the newbie: it is usually pecked at and driven away from the feeder and water. It takes some time for the new hens to take their place in the flock. Therefore, when a new bird is released into the henhouse, you need to carefully monitor the other members' attitudes to take the necessary measures in a timely manner to avoid unpleasant consequences.

LACK OF FEEDERS AND DRINKERS. Stress may occur when there are few feeders and drinkers in the coop. As a result, part of the weakened poultry become malnourished and lose weight; they carry fewer eggs and become unsuitable as producers (although they show no pathological changes at autopsy). To prevent stress, it is necessary to install additional feeders and drinking bowls and arrange them, if possible, as far away as possible from each other.

LOW OR HIGH TEMPERATURES, HIGH HUMIDITY, HIGH LEVELS OF HARMFUL GASES, AND/OR A LOW OXYGEN CONCENTRATION IN THE COOP. Air temperature is one of the most important microclimate parameters. It affects egg production, egg mass and quality, feed intake, body weight, and the overall health of the flock. The optimum temperature in the henhouse for laying hens is considered to be 59–68°F. According to the latest research, a constant temperature at 70°F allows you to get a sufficient number of eggs from poultry and at the same time save more than 14 kg of feed per year for each hen. At high temperatures, if you increase the level of protein and fat in the diet of laying hens, you'll prevent a decrease in their feed intake and increase their egg mass.

Chickens, like all birds in general, tolerate low temperatures more easily than high ones. A temperature between 77–86°F reduces the rate of egg production and feed intake by 1.5%, the weight of eggs by 0.3 g. With a greater increase in air temperature, egg production drops to a minimum and then may stop altogether. The optimum level of relative humidity in the house is 60–65%, but a wider range is also acceptable, from 40 to 70%.

The best indicators of the microclimate level in the coop are the hens' behavior and the state of their plumage. This is especially reflected in the behavior of young animals. With normal humidity, the plumage is smooth and shiny. If the air is dry, feather growth slows down, and the feathers become dry and brittle. Young hens look disheveled and drink a lot of water. With a decrease in humidity to 35–40%, mortality increases. When the coop is damp, the hens are crowded, and their plumage takes on a faded, dirty look.

Good ventilation of the henhouse is one of the most important conditions for keeping and raising chickens. They also need fresh

CAUTION! Chicks should not be grown in the same room as adult livestock. The adult birds' microflora can be fatal to chicks.

air and food. In a well-ventilated room, birds have a good appetite, they are mobile, and they grow faster. In the summer, airing is done by opening the windows closed with a fine mesh, and in the winter using ventilation ducts.

The content of harmful gases should not exceed 0.15–0.18%.

EXTERNAL PARASITES. They can multiply rapidly on the body of hens, lay eggs at the base of feathers or outside the bird — in crevices, holes, and other suitable places. A bird infected with blood-sucking parasites experiences severe itchiness and picks at its feathers with its beak. On the skin of such a bird, you can see abrasions, bald patches, and bite marks, especially in the abdomen, on the back, on the neck, and under the wings.

Parasites suck blood, so birds can refuse food or eat poorly. As a result, they lose weight, egg production decreases, and a hen can even die. Ash baths can help to counter parasites (see more in the "How to Build a Coop -> Equipment and materials for hens flock -> Ash bath" section).

RECAP

★ **Irritants that might provoke stress:**

☆ **A high population density in the coop;**

☆ **Lack of feeders and drinkers;**

☆ **Low or high temperatures, high humidity, high levels of harmful gases, and/or a low oxygen concentration in the coop;**

☆ **External parasites.**

NOTES

EQUIPMENT AND MATERIALS FOR HENS FLOCK

ROOSTS, NESTS, ASH baths, cages, feeders and drinking bowls are the main pieces of equipment you need for chicken houses. These must be durable, simple, and easy to use, clean, and disinfect.

WARMER FOR CHICKS

To heat the young chickens at the beginning of their cultivation, various heating devices can be used. But, unfortunately, many of the popular ones are unsafe and can cause fires.

An example of an effective, cheap, and safe homemade chick warmer.

This can be built in minutes. You need to take a glass liter jar with a plastic lid. Cut a hole in the cover according to the size of the thread of the electric cartridge. The bulb needs to be untwisted from the cartridge, between the upper and lower parts, to insert the lid and then twist it again. You can use a 15–25 W bulb.

Warmer is ready.

DRINKERS

Water should be available to chickens 24 hours a day. An inadequate water supply, in terms of either volume or number of drinking bowls, will reduce the growth rate of your birds. Drinking bowls must be installed at a rate of 8–10 hens per bowl.

Poultry will drink more at higher temperatures. Water consumption increases by about 6.5% by 1.5 degrees Fahrenheit above 70°F. In tropical areas, high temperatures can double water consumption.

In hot weather, you should regularly rinse the drinking bowls to make the water cooler.

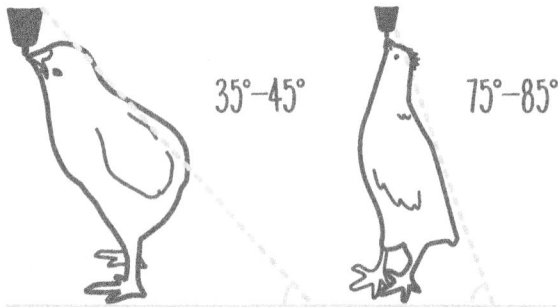

35°–45°   75°–85°

NIPPLE DRINKERS:

The height of the drinkers should be low at the very beginning and increase as the bird grows. Water lines that are too high can reduce water consumption, and water lines that are too low will result in wet litter.

For chicks, the nipple lines must be set to a height that allows the bird to reach the water. The back of the chicken during drinking should be at an angle of 35–45° relative to the floor's surface.

As the bird grows, the nipple lines must be raised so that the back of the bird is at an angle of 75–85 ° to the floor and the bird should slightly reach the water.

BELL DRINKERS:

If you use hanging bell drinkers, then adjust them so that the base of each drinker is no higher than the height of the bird's back. See the figure below.

FEEDERS

In the first ten days, chicks should receive food in the form of sifted grains or mini-granules. Feed must be placed on pallets or spread on paper to ensure chicks have easy access to feed.

The transition to the main feeding system should take place gradually over the course of two to three days as the chickens begin to show interest in the main feeding system.

Basic feeding systems:

CUP FEEDERS (UP TO 15 HENS PER CUP, LESS FOR LARGER POULTRY):

TUBULAR FEEDERS:

All types of feeders must be adjusted to prevent the feed spillage and to ensure optimal poultry access for the feeding bowl. The bottom of the feeder shouldn't be higher than the height as the back of the bird:

CAUTION! At least 25% of the floor surface should be covered with paper.

CAUTION! The incorrect feeding system can increase feed spillage. At the same time, eating spilled food increases risk of bacterial infection.

CAUTION! An uneven feed distribution leads to a decrease in productivity and an increase in damage associated with rivalry for a place at the feeder.

LIFE HACK ALERT! You can keep chickens of any age and type in deep litter.

LITTER

Litter is a poultry housing flooring, based on the repeated spreading of straw or sawdust material. Usually, when laying poultry on the floor, deep litter is used. For bedding material, sawdust, shavings, chopped straw, chopped ears of corn, fallen leaves of trees, peat and other materials can be used. Litter should be dry and shouldn't contain mold.

Lay the litter before getting a new flock and remove it after the end of its maintenance. Change the litter in a coop once a year. During the entire period of keeping, 10–12 kg of litter is consumed per chicken. For young growth, litter is required five to six times less than for adult birds.

In the process of keeping poultry, litter needs to be taken care of. If it is too compact, loosen it, clean wet places, and pour fresh litter.

Under normal conditions, the litter will self-heat and the temperature in its deepest layers will rise to 70°F or more.

Therefore, litter is warm in cold weather. In addition, vitamin B accumulates in the litter material, which has a positive effect on hens.

ROOST

A roost is a rectangular (usually wooden) section where hens sleep. Roosts are made of well-planed bars that do not have knots (a bar can break on a knot). Cross-section of the roost: for chickens — 1.5 × 2.5 inches, for turkeys — 2 × 3 inches.

If the roost is too wide or narrow, the chickens will be uncomfortable when they sleep. Poor rest leads to reduced productivity. The upper edges (ribs) of the roost must definitely be rounded: on sharp edges, the bird can ruin its feet.

If the roosts are long, then they need props for every three to six feet. You cannot place roosts close to the wall: the bird can break its tail that way. Roost length should allow at least six to eight inches per hen. The distance from the wall to the roost should be 12". The height from the floor to the roost should be 35–40".

It's good to place a shield under roosts, which looks like a table. This makes it convenient to remove bird droppings after night from such a shield.

The shield must be made of smoothly planed boards that are well fitted, without gaps. For easy cleaning, finely sprinkle dry peat or sand on the shield.

NESTS

Nest is a box in a henhouse in which domestic chickens lay eggs. Nests are placed in a darkened place so that the poultry can feel calm. The best place to install the nests is near the walls. They should be easily accessible for inspection, egg collection, and cleaning.

Nest sizes for laying hens — 8×12 or 10×12 inches, height — 12"; for broilers — 12×14", height — 14". Also, make the threshold three to four inches high. On average, five chickens per one simple nest. Nests should be made so that the bird willingly visits them.

Nests must be kept clean so as not to contaminate the eggs. In addition, birds don't like to sit in dirty nests. As a nest's litter, wheat straw or wood shavings should be used.

All nests should be thoroughly disinfected twice a year.

ASH BATH

This is a simple but effective means of combating external parasites, which can multiply rapidly on the body of hens, lay eggs at the base of feathers or outside the bird — in crevices, holes, and other suitable places. A bird infected with blood-sucking parasites experiences severe itchiness and picks at its feathers with its beak. On the skin of such a bird, you can see abrasions, bald patches, and bite marks, especially in the abdomen, on the back, on the neck, and under the wings.

Parasites suck blood, so birds can refuse food or eat poorly. As a result, they lose weight, egg production decreases, and a hen can even die.

Ash baths should always be indoors. Place them in a henhouse or aviary under a canopy, in a pit or a wooden box. Constructing an ash bath is simple. You create a mixture of fine, dry sand and wood ash in a ratio of 1:1, and pour that into a box (length — 1 m, height — 10–12 cm). During its scattering, the bath gets replenished.

RECAP

★ Roosts, nests, ash baths, cages, feeders and drinking bowls are the main pieces of equipment you need for chicken houses.

★ It will be nice to have a warmer to heat the young chickens at the beginning of their cultivation.

★ Clean and fresh water should be available to chickens 24 hours a day. The most common drinkers are "Nipple" and "Bell".

★ In the first ten days, chicks should receive food in the form of sifted grains or mini-granules.

★ Feeders must be adjusted to prevent the feed spillage and to ensure optimal poultry access for the feeding bowl. The most common feeders are "Cup" and "Tubular".

★ Litter is a poultry housing flooring, based on the repeated spreading of sawdust, shavings, chopped straw, chopped ears of corn, fallen leaves of trees, peat and other materials.

★ A roost is a rectangular (usually wooden) section where hens sleep which are made of well-planned bars without knots (a bar can break on a knot).

★ Nest is a box in a henhouse in which domestic chickens lay eggs. Nests are placed in a darkened place so that the poultry can feel calm.

★ Ash baths should be in a coop. It is a simple but effective means of combating external parasites.

NOTES

HEALTH AND BIOSECURITY

BIOSECURITY REFERS TO procedures used to prevent the introduction and spread of disease-causing organisms in poultry flocks. It is imperative that farm owners practice daily biosecurity measures. Developing and practicing daily biosecurity procedures will reduce the possibility of introducing infectious diseases, such as Avian Influenza and Exotic Newcastle — among many others.

Poultry are great at masking their symptoms, to prevent themselves from appearing vulnerable to others in the flock. Unfortunately, this means that once symptoms become obvious, it is often too late to treat them successfully.

At the same time, you can keep chickens in the best of health by feeding them a balanced diet containing all the necessary vitamins and minerals, and offer them various natural health-promoting additions, like garlic, cider vinegar, and a range of beneficial herbs and plants. These won't prevent disease but will add to the birds' ability to resist and recover from any diseases that appear in their environment.

By far the best method of biosecurity is to keep your birds as safe from contamination from outside sources as you can. This does not have to be as extreme as practiced by commercial poultry keepers, especially those producing breeding stock for future generations. These more extreme measures include changes of footwear, with designated boots that are never worn outside the poultry shed, or boots that are rigorously scrubbed or dipped in disinfectant before and after entry. Others use disposable overshoes to cover footwear when going inside the poultry shed.

CAUTION! We must not forget that some bird-related diseases are extremely dangerous to humans, such as bird flu and tuberculosis.

DISEASES PREVENTION

How to keep your flock healthy:

1. It's important to isolate new birds from your main flock for a couple of weeks. Have them in a separate quarantine area, as clean as you can make it from contamination, and well away from your other birds.

2. Feed and attend to the new birds after you have attended to your main flock. If the new birds have brought in anything new, this step protects your flock. Also, by attending to them last, you bring in a small amount of the resident 'bug' population

on your hands, hair, clothes and shoes, gradually introducing the new arrivals to what they will meet once they are introduced to the main flock.

3. It takes 2–3 weeks to acquire an immunity to a low level of a new infection, just as it takes around two weeks for immunity to build up following a vaccination.

4. Think about what footwear you wear when moving around your birds, especially around their house and feeding area. Your footwear is probably the biggest source of infection, transporting bugs in the muck contained in the tread from one place to another. Ideally, wear boots specifically for feeding the hens, and clean them thoroughly each time.

5. Do not wear the same boots to visit a neighbour's chicken run, or to go traipsing through the duck poo at the park or down by the creek, or even to visit the local poultry show. Even walking through your local farm store, feed merchant or sale yards, where someone else with a flock has walked before in their mucky boots, can be a risk. The muck you gather can drop off once you get home and be a source of new, unwelcome bugs to your birds.

6. Buy a good pair of gumboots with as little tread as possible so it's easy to scrub them clean, and always dunk them in a disinfectant. You can't decontaminate dirt with disinfectant so the boots must be scrubbed clean first.

7. The bottoms of buckets, forks and shovels may also carry contamination. That's not so bad within your own flock, but it pays to make sure these things are clean if you have lots of young birds. Visit chicks and young birds first, before you go into a run with adult birds.

8. Don't re-use equipment like buckets, or the brush that you use for cleaning, between new or young birds and your main flock.

9. Wild birds, rodents and other livestock can be carriers of diseases which may not affect that species but will infect poultry. Set traps for rats, stoats and mice as populations can escalate with the ready availability of food. Pick up uneaten scraps of food which can attract vermin, endeavour to keep sparrows and other birds out of feeders by having them closed when not in use, or keep them in a sparrow-proof shed (feed hens inside).

Although the risk of a disease is low, for the sake of your flock health, if you practice good, everyday biosecurity, you are protecting their health.

THE MOST COMMON CHICKEN DISEASES YOU SHOULD KNOW ABOUT (AND HOW TO TREAT THEM)

1. FOWL POX

If you notice that your chickens develop white spots on their skin, scabby sores on their combs, white ulcers in their mouth or trachea, and their laying stops then you should grow concerned that your chickens are developing Fowl Pox.

There are treatment options for Fowl Pox. You can feed them soft food and give them a warm and dry place to try and recoup. With adequate care, there is a great chance that your birds can survive this illness.

If you would like to remove the odds of your birds even contracting this disease there is a vaccine available. If not, know that they can contact this disease from other contaminated chickens, mosquitos, and it is a virus so it can be contracted by air as well.

2. BOTULISM

If your chickens begin to have progressing tremors you should grow concerned. If your chickens have botulism the tremors will progress into total body paralysis which does include their breathing.

It is a serious disease.

You will also notice their feathers will be easy to pull out and death usually occurs within a few hours.

But what can you do about it?

Well, there is an antitoxin that can be purchased from your local vet. Though it is considered to be expensive. However, if you catch the disease early enough you can mix I teaspoon of Epsom salts with I ounce of warm water. You can give it to them by dropper once daily.

If your chickens have contracted this disease it means that there has been some type of dead meat left near their food and water which contaminated it. Which means this disease is avoidable as long as you keep your chickens in a clean environment and clean up any dead carcass from around their environment.

3. FOWL CHOLERA

You should be suspicious of this disease if you see your birds begin to have a greenish or yellowish diarrhea, are having obvious joint pain, are struggling to breathe, and have a darkened head or wattle. Fowl Cholera is a bacterial disease that can be contracted from wild animals or food and water that has been contaminated by this bacteria.

But the downside to your chicken developing this disease is there is no real treatment. If by some chance your chicken survives, it will still always be a carrier of the disease.

So it is usually better to put them down and destroy their carcass so it will not be passed.

But there is a vaccine for your chickens to prevent the disease from ever taking hold.

Signs Equate Fowl Cholera

Swellings of comb and wattles

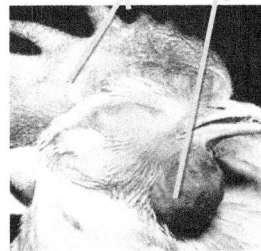

Mouth and nasal discharge

4. INFECTIOUS BRONCHITIS

This disease hits close to home because it wiped out half of our flock when we were new to raising chickens. You'll recognize this disease when you begin to hear your chickens sneezing, snoring, and coughing. And then the drainage will begin to secrete from their nose and eyes.

Their laying will cease too.

But the good news is you can get a vaccine to stop this disease from impacting your chickens.

However, if you decide against that then you will need to move quickly when seeing these signs. Infectious Bronchitis is a viral disease and will travel quickly through the air.

To treat Infectious Bronchitis, give your chickens a warm, dry place to recoup. I gave my birds a warm herb tea and fed them fresh herbs, which seemed to help.

5. INFECTIOUS CORYZA

You will know that your birds have caught this disease when their heads become swollen. Their eyes will literally swell shut and their combs will swell. Then the discharge will begin to flow from their eyes and noses. They will stop laying and will have moisture under their wings.

Unfortunately, there is no vaccine to stop this disease.

Once your chickens contract this disease they should be put down. If not, they will remain a carrier of the disease for life which is a risk to the rest of your flock.

Be sure to discard the body afterward so no other animal becomes infected by it.

However, the light at the end of this tunnel is that even though this disease is a bacteria it only travels through contaminated water, other contaminated birds, and surfaces that have been contaminated with the bacteria.

So if you keep your chickens protected from other random chickens and keep their coop and water clean they should be safe from this disease.

6. MAREK'S DISEASE

This disease is more common in younger birds that are usually under the age of 20 weeks.

So you will know that this disease has struck your baby chicks if you begin to see tumors growing inside or outside of your chick. Their iris will turn gray and they will no longer respond to light. And they will become paralyzed.

Unfortunately, this disease is very easy for them to catch. It is a virus which means it is super easy to transmit from bird to bird. They actually obtain the virus by breathing in pieces of shed skin and feather from an infected chick.

And sadly, if your chick gets this disease it needs to be put down. It will remain a carrier of the disease for life if it survives.

However, the good news is there is a vaccine and it is usually given to day old chicks.

7. THRUSH

Thrush with chickens is very similar to thrush that babies get.

You'll notice a white oozy substance inside their crop (which is a space between their neck and body). They will have a larger than normal appetite. The chicken will appear lethargic and have a crusty vent area. And their feathers will look ruffled.

It is important to mention that thrush is a fungal disease. This means it can be contracted if you allow your chickens to eat molded feed or other molded food. And they can also contract the disease from contaminated water or surfaces.

Though there is no vaccine, it can be treated by an anti-fungal medicine that you can get from your local vet. Be sure to remove the bad food and clean their water container as well.

8. AIR SAC DISEASE

This disease first appears in the form of poor laying skills and a weak chicken. As it progresses, you will notice coughing, sneezing, breathing problems, swollen joints, and possibly death.

Now, there is a vaccine for this illness, and it can be treated with an antibiotic from the vet. But it can be picked up from other birds (even wild birds) and it can be transferred from a hen that has it to her chick through the egg.

So just keep an eye out for any of these symptoms so it can be treated quickly and effectively.

9. NEWCASTLE DISEASE

This disease also appears through the respiratory system. You will begin to see breathing problems, discharge from their nose, their eyes will begin to look murky, and their laying will stop. Also, it is common that the bird's legs and wings will become paralyzed as well as their necks twisted.

This disease is carried by other birds including wild birds. That is how it is usually contracted. But if you touch an infected bird you can pass it on from your clothes, shoes, and other items.

However, the good news is that older birds usually will recover and they are not carriers afterward.

But most baby birds will die from the disease.

There is a vaccine for the disease though the US is working to rid the country of the disease all the way around.

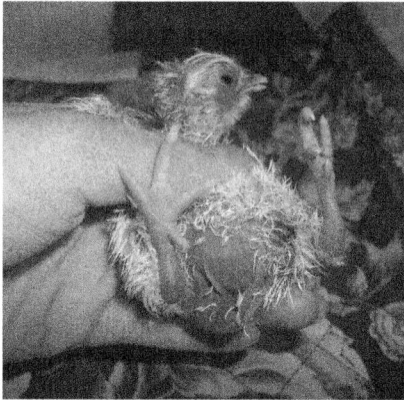

10. MUSHY CHICK

This disease obviously will impact chicks. It usually shows up in newly hatched chicks that have a midsection that is enlarged, inflamed, and blue tinted. The chick will have an unpleasant scent and will appear to be drowsy. Naturally, the chick will also be weak.

So this disease doesn't have a vaccine. It usually is transmitted from chick to chick or from a dirty surface where an infected chick was. And usually, it is contracted from an unclean area where a chick with a weak immune system contracts the bacteria.

There is no vaccine for this disease, although sometimes antibiotics will work. But usually, when you come in contact with this disease you will need to immediately separate your healthy chicks from the sick ones.

Use caution as the bacteria within this disease (such as staph and strep) can impact humans.

11. PULLORUM

This disease impacts chicks and older birds differently. The chicks will show no signs of activity, have a white paste all over their backsides, and show signs of breathing difficulty. Though some will die with no signs at all.

However, in older birds, you will see sneezing and coughing on top of poor laying skills.

This is a viral disease. It can be contracted through contaminated surfaces and other birds that have become carriers of the disease. Unfortunately, there is no vaccine for this disease and all birds that contract the disease should be put down and the carcass destroyed so no other animal will pick up the disease.

12. AVIAN INFLUENZA

Avian Influenza is most commonly known as the bird flu. It was one of my initial fears of owning chickens because all you hear about on the news is how people get sick with bird flu from their chickens. However, after knowing the symptoms you'll be able to put that fear to rest.

You need to know how to act quickly if you are afraid your backyard birds have come in contact with it.

So the signs you will notice will include respiratory troubles. Your chickens will quit laying. They will probably develop diarrhea. You may notice swelling in your chicken's face and that their comb and wattle are discolored or have turned blue.

And they may even develop dark red spots on their legs and combs.

Unfortunately, there is no vaccine and the chickens infected will always be carriers. Wild animals can even carry the disease from bird to bird.

Once your birds get this disease, they need to be put down and the carcass destroyed. And you will need to sanitize any area that the birds were in before ever introducing a new flock.

Use great caution because this disease can make humans sick.

And here is a great resource about avian influenza for all backyard chicken keepers. Hopefully, this will help to put your mind at rest about this disease and your backyard flock.

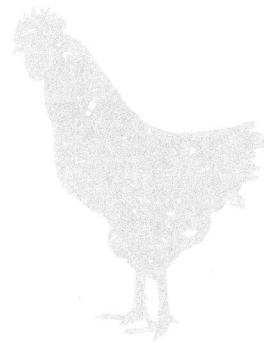

13. BUMBLEFOOT

Bumblefoot is a disease that you'll know exactly what you're looking at when you see it.

It begins by your chicken accidentally cutting its foot on something. It can happen when they are digging in the garden, scratching around in mulch, and so many other ways. But then

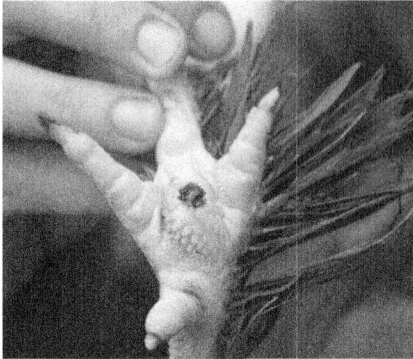

the cut gets infected. And the chicken's foot will begin to swell. It can even swell up the leg.

So you can treat it by performing surgery (learn how here). If not, the infection will eventually take over the chicken and claim its life.

Obviously, bumblefoot can happen very easily and there isn't much you can do to prevent besides just keep a close eye on your chickens' feet. If you notice they have a cut then be sure to wash and disinfect it to prevent this disease from setting up.

That is all of the common chicken diseases.

However, there are many less common illnesses too. So just be sure to always pay attention to your flock and stay alert to any changes. Never be afraid to research. It is better to overreact than to underreact and miss something that could be detrimental to your whole flock.

RECAP

★ Some bird's diseases are extremely dangerous for humans, such as bird flu and tuberculosis. Follow these 9 simple rules to keep your flock healthy:

☆ Isolate new birds from your main flock for a couple of weeks.

☆ Feed and attend to the new birds after you have attended to your main flock.

☆ It takes 2–3 weeks to acquire an immunity to a low level of a new infection. Keep it in mind if you follow a vaccination.

☆ Your footwear is probably the biggest source of infection. Wear boots specifically for feeding the hens if it's possible.

☆ Do not wear the same boots for your and neighbour's chicken run.

☆ Buy a good pair of gumboots with as little tread as possible so it's easy to scrub them clean, and always dunk them in a disinfectant.

☆ The bottoms of buckets, forks and shovels may also carry contamination.

☆ Don't re-use equipment like buckets, or the brush that you use for cleaning, between new or young birds and your main flock.

☆ Wild birds, rodents and other livestock can be carriers of diseases which may not affect that species but will infect poultry.

★ The Most Common Chicken Diseases:

☆ Fowl Pox

☆ Botulism

☆ Fowl Cholera

☆ Infectious Bronchitis

☆ Infectious Coryza

☆ Marek's Disease

☆ Thrush

☆ Air Sac Disease

☆ Newcastle Disease

☆ Mushy Chick

☆ Pullorum

☆ Avian Influenza

☆ Bumblefoot.

NOTES

NOTES

COUNCILS
OF SKILLED
POULTRYMAN

POULTRY INSTINCTS

WHY DO HENS STOP LAYING EGGS

A pause in egg laying can be caused by a sharp weather change, a strong fright, a lack of nutrients in the diet, molting, and various diseases. A lack of protein in the diet or poor-quality feed (moldy, salty, rotten, etc.) usually leads to a gradual decrease in egg-laying, too.

When birds begin their natural seasonal molting or artificial molting caused by starvation, they can stop laying eggs for up to two months. After that, egg production is usually restored.

Common decorative breeds of chickens, turkeys, ducks, and geese at the end of the breeding season usually show their hatching instinct. During this period, they stop laying eggs. Hens stop laying eggs with severe diseases, especially those associated with impaired sexual function.

HOW TO STOP HEN'S HATCHING INSTINCT

If you're keeping a large flock, the usually manifested incubation instinct is not always desirable. In order to prevent this phenomenon, hens that start hatching should be placed in a specially made cage with a mesh floor. Give the hens in the cage protein-rich food and clean water.

The cage should be placed in a well-lit, cool place. After 1–1.5 weeks, such a bird stops hatching and begins to lay eggs. The most important thing in this matter is to seize the moment at the very beginning of the hatching and to isolate the hen in a timely manner. If you miss the beginning of the moment, the technique described above may not succeed.

WHY DO SOME BROODY HENS STOP INCUBATION?

Good sitter hens are turkeys, geese, musky ducks, and hens of common breeds. But even a good hen, if you don't follow the rules for caring, feeding, and drinking, can stop incubation.

Most often, a brood hen stops incubating if something bothers her (for example, when the nests are located in a cold room, in a highly lit area, or in passages where she often feels scared, next to other animals).

During the incubation period, it is necessary to provide for the possibility of the hens coming off the nests for feeding and watering. In this case, separate their feeders and drinking bowls.

CHICKEN FERTILIZERS

VALUABLE ORGANIC FERTILIZER

It is well known that chicken manure is a valuable concentrated organic fertilizer. It contains all the elements necessary for plant nutrition in a favorable amount.

In terms of the crop effect, chicken droppings are closer to mineral fertilizers than to manure. But its consequences are favorable in comparison with mineral fertilizers since part of the nitrogen in it is in organic form and is constantly turning into a state that's accessible to plants.

In addition, the use of poultry droppings increases the activity of microbiological processes in the soil and provides a stable yield increase for two to three years.

HOW TO FERTILIZE SOIL WITH CHICKEN DROPPINGS

It is possible and useful to fertilize soil with chicken droppings, if there is such an opportunity. But this must be done competently, in a timely manner, following the recommendations tested by practice:

★ Do not bring in large quantities of fresh manure to the soil, because it dries quickly and there will be no benefit from it.

★ It is undesirable to use manure found in poultry farms—there is a lot of sawdust in that manure, and when it rots in the soil, it emits a lot of nitrogen, thereby taking nutrients from plants. It is best to make liquid manure from chicken droppings.

★ After plant nutrition, the plant can be overlaid with weeds, mowed lawn grass, straw, or needles. In this case, there will be no bad smell or flies in the area.

HOW TO HUMANELY KILL A CHICKEN

The hen must be carefully prepared for slaughter in order to facilitate the plucking of feathers and fluff and to extend the shelf life of the meat. Through pre-slaughter fasting, the gastrointestinal tract is freed from food and feces. Chickens stop feeding 18–24 hours before slaughter. Ten hours before slaughter, the water supply should be cut off. During this period, the bird should be kept in a cage or box with a trellised or mesh floor, so that it doesn't peck at the litter and ground.

Use a very sharp knife for slaughter. You can either have someone hold the chicken upside down, pinning her wings, or use a kill cone.

Slice the knife across her throat directly under the chin on either side of her larynx. Make one cut parallel to her jaw bone on each side. This slices the arteries rather than the trachea.

If you cut straight across the center of the throat, you have to go deeper with the knife, which will kill her more slowly and cause more pain.

The knife should be very sharp. The sharpest knife you've ever handled. When you are killing an animal, the sharper the blade, the more painless and humane the death. A knife sharp enough to kill with should have an edge that drags at your skin like raw silk when you put the ball of your thumb against its edge. If your finger slides easily, without cutting you, it is too dull. The knife blade should be trying to slice your flesh with the barest pressure, and it will feel rough or "sticky" like the very fine spikes on a burr. Always sharpen your knife between every couple of kills.

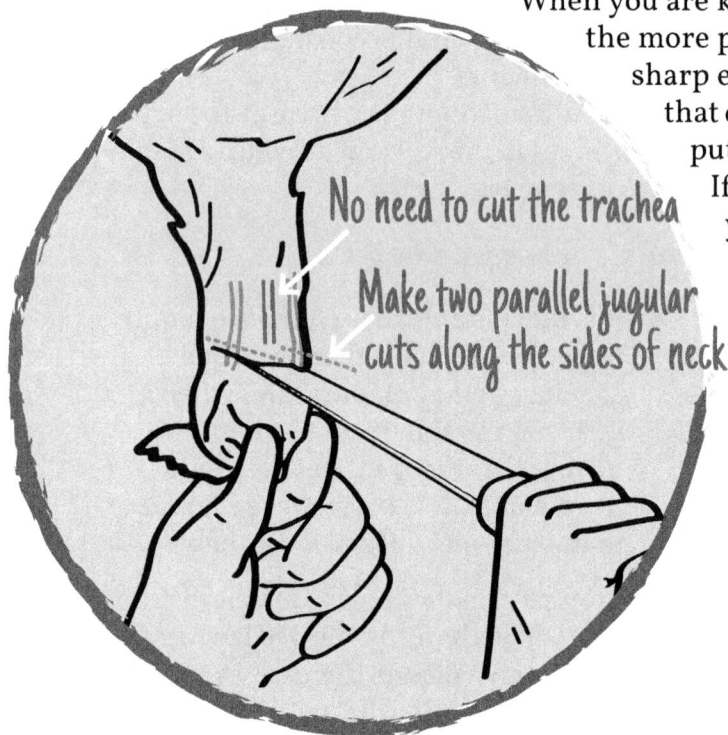

No need to cut the trachea

Make two parallel jugular cuts along the sides of neck

CLEAN AND PROCESSING FOR FOOD

Once a chicken is dead, you have a second task — processing the chicken so it can be cooked.

First, you scald the chicken to make the feathers easier to pluck. Use a pot of water at 140 degrees F. Too hot and the chicken will start to cook. Too cool, and the feathers won't become loose.Dunk the chicken for about 15 to 20 seconds and remove. The feathers should come off easily in handfuls.

Have two buckets ready — an offal bucket for waste and a clean bucket for edible organs. Of the organs, you can save the heart, liver, gizzard, and testicles of an adult rooster. Male birds killed at the usual age of meat birds have not developed testicles yet, but if you are killing an older rooster, you will find sizable testicles that have a mild flavor and spongy texture.

Once the chicken is defeathered, use your knife to remove the chicken's head, if your slaughter method didn't do that alrcady. Thcn start the evisceration at the cloaca, with another sharp knife.

Cut in a circle around the opening of the cloaca and tie the end of the intestines to prevent feces coming out as you pull. Gently pull the guts out, using your fingers or a knife to carefully separate the membranes attaching them to the body cavity.

After the guts, you take out the other organs. Most come out easily, although sometimes you have to scrape the deflated lungs off the rib cage.

The next two steps are important, but easy to forget. First, you must remove the oil gland or sac at the base of the tail, which produces a smelly, sticky grease. It is an unpleasant surprise to accidentally puncture that sac on a cooked chicken, so cut it out with your knife while gutting.

The second thing to remember, and what I find to be the most technically challenging part of gutting a chicken, is to remove the crop. The crop is a small, nubby part of the esophagus above the gizzard which stores food. It is the last thing you pull out of a chicken.

You just have to get a grip on the esophagus, which is slippery, and pull hard. Some people remove it from the top of the neck. I was taught to remove it from the bottom, after the other organs have been removed.

The final step is to remove the chicken's feet, which cut off easily at the knee muscle. The scaly skin peels off the feet, leaving them clean and ready to cook.

HOW TO CUT A WHOLE CHICKEN

Whole chickens are good for roasting, but you can also cut them into pieces for braises and stews — and they cost about a dollar less than precut chickens. Tip: Don't throw away the leftover back and neck. Store them in the freezer each time you cut a chicken until you have enough for stock. Simmer for an hour with water to cover, and you'll have a base for a great soup.

STEP 1. With the chicken breast facing up, pull each leg away from the body, then slice through the skin between the breast and drumstick.
Tip: A sharp chef's knife makes cutting easier, and a separate cutting board for meat helps avoid cross-contamination. These steps also work for cooked chicken.

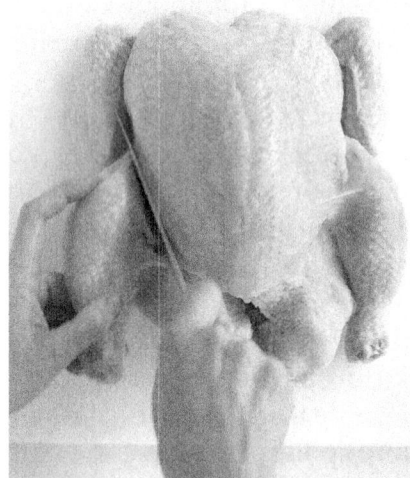

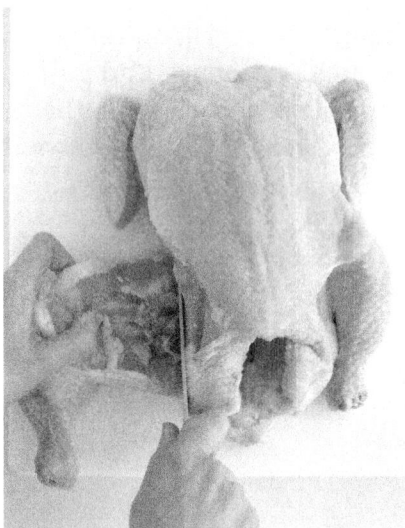

STEP 2. Turn the chicken on its side. Bend each leg back until the thigh-bone pops out of its socket. Cut through joint and skin to detach each leg completely.

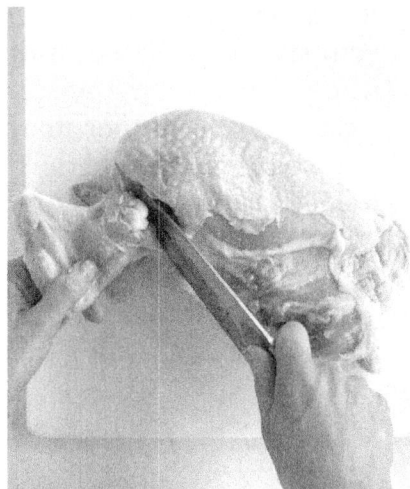

STEP 3. With the chicken on its side, pull each wing away from the body. Cut through the joint and remove each wing.

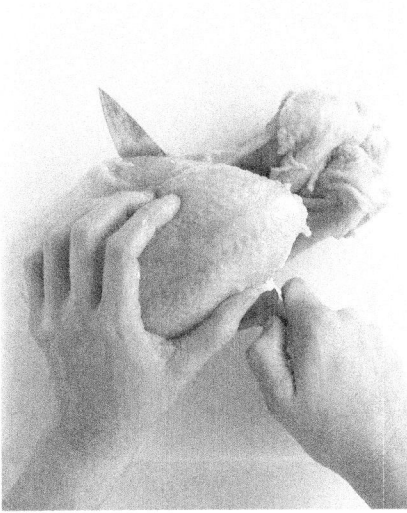

STEP 4. Lift the chicken and cut downward through its rib cage and then its shoulder joints to separate breast from back (save the back for stock).

STEP 5. Turn the chicken over, so the breast is face down. Split the center bone with a chopping motion, then slice through the meat and skin to separate into two pieces.

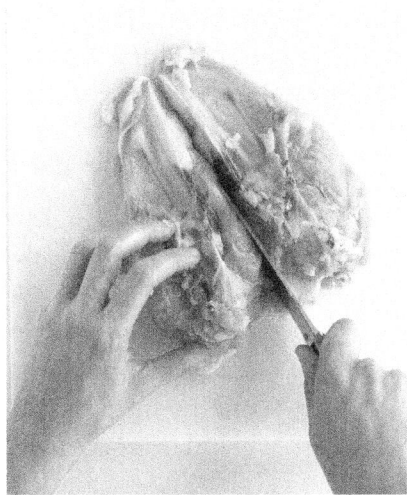

STEP 6. To cut the breast halves into quarters, make sure the skin is facing upward and cut in half diagonally through bone.

STEP 7. To divide the legs, make sure the skin is facing downward and cut through the joints (along the white fat line) to separate thigh from drumstick.

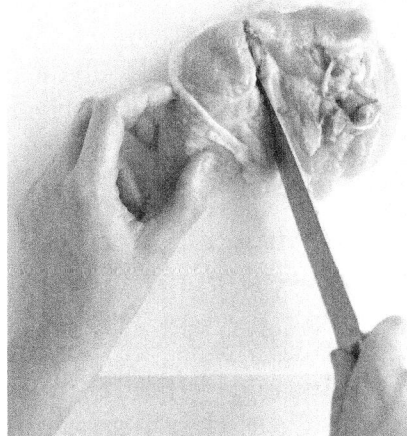

You should end up with six to ten parts, depending on whether or not you divided the breast and legs into halves.

HOW TO HANDLE AND STORAGE EGGS PROPERLY

The average egg in the grocery store can be up to 8 weeks old by the time you buy it. Hopefully none of your backyard eggs will hang around that long, but if they do, here are some tips to keeping your eggs fresh as long as possible.

KEEP THE EGGS CLEAN

Nesting box bedding should be changed often so it is always clean and eggs should be collected as often as possible. That way the eggs should be clean and not caked with mud or chicken poop.

If any eggs are too dirty, rinse them immediately with warm water (cool water can cause bacteria to be pulled into the egg through the pores in the shell) and scramble them up for our dog or to feed back to the chickens, but grind them carefully before. They are a super nutritious treat for the chickens.

DON'T WASH THEM

As a general rule, eggs should not be washed immediately after collecting them. There is a natural bloom on the surface of the shell that keeps out air and bacteria. Its important to leave the bloom intact in order to keep your eggs fresh.

LIFE HACK ALERT! Eggs separate better if they are cold, but whites will beat higher and stiffer if they are allowed to sit at room temperature for at least 30 minutes.

ONE DAY OUT AT ROOM IS EQUIVALENT TO A WEEK IN THE REFRIGERATOR

If you aren't planning on eating your eggs for awhile, it is best to refrigerate them. They will keep about seven times longer.

PROPER STORAGE

Eggs should always be stored with the pointy end down and the blunt end up. The air sac in the blunt end helps keep additional moisture from being lost. Since eggshells are porous and will absorb odors, they should be stored in a carton or covered container. A bowl with plastic wrap over the top works fine in a pinch.

FREEZE THE EXTRAS

Eggs also freeze well, so I always freeze any extra eggs during the summer and fall to use through the winter when production drops. If you live in a cold climate, there's a danger of the eggs freezing outside in the nesting boxes and possibly cracking, so try to collect your eggs more frequently.

NOT SURE IF AN EGG IS GOOD?

If you are in doubt as to how old an egg is, just do the 'Float Test'. Drop the egg into a glass of water. A fresh egg will lay on the bottom of the glass. An egg that is two to three weeks old will start to rise up off the bottom of the glass. It is still perfectly good to eat, just not quite as fresh. It will also hard boil better/peel easier, but I steam eggs instead — that way I can use freshly laid eggs and not have to wait for our eggs to 'age' to peel easily.

An egg that is two months old will start to angle up a bit more and by three months will stand up straight in the glass, but as long as one end is still touching the bottom, it's still perfectly good to eat. If an egg floats, it's very old and could be bad. I would toss it.

Still fresh   Still fresh, but should be used soon   No longer fresh and should be discarded

POULTRY SUPERSTITIONS

★ Eggs for hatching are usually laid on Wednesdays, Fridays, or Saturdays and always in the evening. It is not known where this tradition came from, but it has been repeatedly tested. The hatching of chicks is, as a rule, better if you adhere to these unwritten rules.

★ Feed chickens chopped eggshells (to strengthen the skeleton). But be careful — add only a little bit to the main feed mixture, and the eggshell should be maximally chopped. It's possible that adding many eggshells to a chicken's diet is the cause of "cannibalism" in chickens. Especially if the shell is given without chopping it first.

★ To strengthen the hen's body and increase resistance to infections in the winter, it is necessary to give chickens, in addition to mineral top dressing (chalk, bone meal, shell), fish oil.

★ Experienced poultry breeders replace roosters once every two to three years to improve the heredity of the chicken flock. They do not take a rooster of their own, but always from other farms so that there is not even a distant relationship. And in order not to disturb the hens, the substitution is carried out at night.

CHICKENS AND THE WEATHER:

★ The rooster begins to sing intensely at "inopportune" times before the weather changes;

★ Hens pluck themselves and grease feathers before severe weather conditions;

★ Before a frost, chickens perch early;

★ The rooster sings at the wrong time in the summer (for rain) and in winter (for warmth);

★ A hen that looks disheveled may signal bad weather;

★ If hens don't hide from the rain, the rain will last long.

RECAP:

★ Don't wash your eggs until just before you are ready to use them. Once you have removed the 'bloom', you have removed the protective barrier against air and bacteria.

★ Unwashed eggs will last at least two weeks unrefrigerated and three months or more in the refrigerator.

★ If the eggs are soiled and MUST be washed, use warm water and try to use them immediately or at least refrigerate them right away.

★ Washed eggs will last at least 2 months in the refrigerator but won't taste as fresh as unwashed eggs of the same age.

★ When in doubt, do the float test before using the egg.

NOTES

CONCLUSION

POULTRY BREEDING IS quite an extensive topic, and my book should serve as a good guide for you. If you read it carefully, then you know more than enough about successfully raising and keeping chickens. With a little patience and effort, you'll get a great backyard flock!

I tried to explain this topic in as much detail as possible, but if you have questions, feel free email me here: matthew.bawerman@gmail.com. I'll be happy to help you, and I promise answer to each one of your questions. I'll also be grateful to hear any feedback you have about the book and meet fellow chicken breeders around the world.

If you enjoyed it, then please consider leaving a review on Amazon.

Thank you!

Printed in Great Britain
by Amazon